Away From the Light of Day

Amadou and Mariam
with Idrissa Keïta

Translated by Ann Wright

route

First published in 2010 by Route
PO Box 167, Pontefract, WF8 4WW
info@route-online.com
www.route-online.com

ISBN (13): 978-1-901927-45-0
ISBN (10): 1-901927-45-8

Originally published in French
© Michel Lafon Publishing, 2008 *À part la lumière du jour*

Cover photograph: Youri Lenquette
Cover Design: Golden www.wearegolden.co.uk

Amadou and Mariam would like to sincerely thank:
Marc-Antoine Moreau, Thierry Langlois, Manu Chao,
Mathieu Chedid, Because Record Company.

Idrissa Keïta thanks the Good Lord, his mother, feue Hadja Rokia
Keïta, may her soul rest in peace, his father, El hadji Siriman Keïta, his
ancestors, may their souls rest in peace, Annette Keïta, Fanta 'Sibika'
Keïta, Amadou 'Adou' Sangaré, Margaret, Sylvianne, Boubacar Marega
and Nathalie, Ibrahima 'Vieux' Keïta, Aminata Keïta, Awa 'Matjola'
Keïta, Koman Keïta, Makam Keïta, Sidiki Keïta. All parents and
friends who recognise themselves in these pages.

Printed by CPI Bookmarque, Croydon

Route is supported by Arts Council England

Away From the Light of Day

Chapter One
The White of My Eyes

They say I was born on 24 October 1954, in Bamako, the capital of Mali. It was a beautiful day apparently, typical of the end of the rainy season. I was born, and with me my illness – a congenital cataract in each eye – and with my illness, the rumours. For here in Mali, it's not modern medicine that has the last word. My mother told me later that she was asked if, as well as praying, she had offered sacrifices to the ancestors as protection for her baby. When a baby comes into the world with milky eyes like me, they try to understand why.

My uncle on my father's side, the late Fodé Bangali Bagayogo, was also a target for the gossips. A fearsome hunter, he was warned of the catastrophes he might unleash on himself and his family by killing animals. Animals have a privileged bond with the Creator, with God, and possess extraordinary powers. They have the gift of damning or blessing you and nothing in the world is worse than the evil eye of animals. People also reminded Fodé that he had to be careful not to commit the unpardonable, like mistaking for game an animal searching for food to feed its young. Hence, certain people began to suspect my uncle of having something to do with my illness. As if my milky eyes were proof of his sin.

These superstitious causes of my cataracts did not interest my late father, Ibrahima Bagayogo. He believed in doctors' diagnoses and their scientific explanations. Back then, he never imagined I'd be completely blind one day and that he'd have to take my hand and lead me wherever I wanted to go. He didn't imagine it because he didn't want to imagine it: in those days being blind was the worst calamity that could happen to you in Malian society. It was tantamount to being a beggar. No two ways about it, a blind person depended on others, on their charity. Everything a blind person has, he gets out of pity.

When I was little, my cataracts were in their early stages, so it didn't stop me seeing. I didn't see very well, but I did see. Hospitals in Mali lacked the amenities to perform the type of operation my eyes needed. And even if they did have them, my father couldn't have afforded it. As a bricklaying instructor, he barely earned enough to cover his family's needs. So I was stuck with my cataracts.

My childhood wasn't all that hard, at least not compared to my father's. When he was very young, he left his native village of Torakoroni, in the Bougouni region, in the south of Mali. He really had no choice. He knew there was no future for him in Torakoroni. In Bamako, on the other hand, he hoped to make his way in the world. He became a bricklaying instructor, a trade he plied all his life. He also met my mother in Bamako and they got married. My mother, the late Mariam Diarra, was from Quélékoro, a village just fifteen kilometres from Bamako, in the Kati region, in western Mali. She was a full-time mother. She looked after us all her life. It wouldn't be exaggerating to call her a 'plenipotentiary housewife'. In our family she took all the decisions, managed the rhythm and running of everyday life, and educated us. She reigned over a veritable tribe. I am the second, after my sister Aminata Bagayogo, of the fourteen children she brought into the world, and the first boy. Two boys, Moussa and Tiguida, died. Now, there are the same number of girls as boys.

The year Mali declared its independence on 22 September 1960, President Modibo Keïta's socialist government began a campaign to tackle unemployment and illiteracy. It created various public services in Bamako and other regions. One of them was known as the Civic Service, a sort of military and civil education scheme. My father joined up. Recruits first went through an obligatory six-month military training; those who didn't want to become soldiers were free to choose other professions which were also taught as part of the programme.

In the early years of independence, Bamako was still quite a small place. The rural exodus had not yet started. The countryside was very populated while the capital had barely half a million inhabitants. Malians were mostly engaged in agriculture, raising cattle, and construction work. The Civic Service sent its people throughout Mali, especially into the villages, to spread word of the scheme and encourage people to join up. That's how my father was recruited and sent to Bamako. He learned his trade there and ended up teaching bricklaying to both soldiers and civilians.

In Mali, community life is founded on strict rituals. For example, when a young man of the village who has moved to town or emigrated to another country wants to get married, he has to come back and introduce his wife to his family and the whole community. The bridegroom also has to obey certain Malian customs which vary from village to village, and region to region. In my father's case, he had to come back to Torakoroni with his wife, and kneel under the old village trees, to honour God, the benign village spirits and the ancestors. This ritual was supposed to dispel bad luck and guarantee our family's happiness.

So my father brought my mother to Torakoroni to introduce her to his parents, his relatives and the benign village spirits. I was two years old and my mother had not wanted to leave me behind. So I was there for the big feast that the village chief had organised in their honour. He had invited all the well-known local musicians to form an orchestra and play for the whole day. I remember the music as if it were yesterday.

Of all the instruments I heard, the one that impressed me most apparently was the tam-tam. I cried during the whole ceremony to be allowed to play it. It was the first time I'd seen the instrument. That day was a turning point for me. I developed a profound interest in music which gradually turned into an exclusive passion. Since then, not a single day of my life has passed without music.

My attraction to the tam-tam amused the musicians, so much so that they decided to make one for me, a small-scale version, to take back to Bamako. I made good use of it.

The profession of musician in Mali is reserved for the caste of bards, troubadours, storytellers, known as *griots*. In those days, they were the guardians of customs and traditions, the living libraries of West Africa. Even today, they assume the role of mediators, counsellors, and see to it that marriages work out or conflicts within a community don't get out of hand. Certain conservative Malians, who are not part of the *griot* caste, forbid their children to play instruments or make music their profession.

This system of caste prevents individuals developing and nurturing their vocation. I think culture should evolve with the times, like everything else, and do away with archaic practices. It seems nonsensical that such a division still exists in Mali, and that talent can be wasted because of it. Thank God my father was liberal and let me play the tam-tam with all my heart and soul, and sing to the rhythms I invented. My paternal grandfather was tolerant too, and he let my uncle, Fodé Bangali, play the *dosso n'goni*, literally 'the hunters' guitar', a sort of skin-covered gourd with a string bow.

The year I turned eight, in 1962, my father was posted to the CAR camp (rural training centre) in Kita, a town on the railway line from Bamako to Dakar, the capital of Senegal. It was in Kita that my father first enrolled me in school. Despite my disability, I could follow lessons like the other children. I just had to sit in the front row so I could see the blackboard. I always took my tam-tam to school and played it at break times. A crowd would always gather around me and I ended up with a little audience of classmates who admired and encouraged me.

Our family stayed in Kita for three years until my father got another posting, this time to the CAR training camp in Douansan, a town in the north of Mali on the edge of the

Sahara desert, about 800 kilometres from Bamako. It is in the Mopti region, an area very well irrigated by several tributaries of the Niger River. Some flow around Douansan, others pass through the town and provide it with drinking water and fresh fish, the trade of which is the main commercial activity of the region.

In those days, five years after independence, Mali still lacked adequate infrastructure. There were only a few good paved roads, the rest of the road network was in a terrible state. The journey from Kito to Douansan took three days. We had to take the train to Bamako, then get pick-up trucks-cum-buses called 'bush-taxis' for the rest of the journey. This transport was slow and, above all, expensive.

My father's meagre salary barely covered food, clothes and school fees. So we could only take the strict minimum of belongings with us to Douansan, and my tam-tam was not included. My father promised to buy me a harmonica and an African flute. I agreed although I'd never played either instrument. And I was happy to learn. I picked them up pretty quickly and practised at break time and in the holidays. Practising at school made me quite popular, I'd play and my schoolmates would dance and clap. Grown-ups looked on admiringly as well, and the girls started giving me the eye. I enjoyed my mini-idol status.

Chapter Two
The Hand of Fate

As my audience grew, my sight failed. My cataracts had begun to affect my eyes badly and my eyesight deteriorated. After dark, it became difficult for me to get about without help. My parents were very worried. In Douansan the street-lighting was so dim that the town was plunged into almost total darkness from sunset. When there was no moon, people needed torches, and to play in the street we children gathered round a petrol lamp. We'd play until it was too chilly to stay outside. I liked being with kids my own age but I couldn't go out and play with them unless a friend came for me and took me home afterwards. I began to feel very unhappy about being so dependent. I refused to accept what was happening, that I would always need other people.

In Mali, the dry season begins in November and lasts until the first rains come at the end of May, or the beginning of June. A drop in the river level signals the start of the festive season in the villages. The high point of the festivities is when the whole village goes fishing together. I was lucky enough to be part of this collective fish for the first time in Douansan, where fishing is done in a traditional way with rudimentary implements. The catch is divided into two, one half for eating and the other to sell.

I had heard so much about the festival that I was dying to take part. When the long-awaited day arrived, I wanted to go into the river with the others and get close to the fish. But my father advised against it, arguing that the water was too churned up by all the fishermen chasing the biggest fish. When I insisted he said, 'Even men whose eyesight is one hundred per cent perfect risk getting hurt. You can hardly see anything, it's best you don't go.' Until then I hadn't really been conscious of being less able than the others. I didn't realise how disabled I was, or rather I didn't want to accept it. I felt like crying. Standing by and watching my friends fishing in the river was so frustrating. That's when I got really worried, I resented what this cruel illness was stealing from my life.

I went into my bedroom. Sitting on the bed, I put my head in my hands. I didn't know what to do. I didn't want to disobey my father but neither did I want to stand on the bank watching my friends fishing. Then I thought of going back with my flute. A huge crowd of men was moving towards the river. Only women, young children, old people and the very ill had stayed at home, and some men in charge of village security. It was very hot. The reflection of the sun's rays on the water made the naked torsos sparkle. In the shade of a huge baobab tree, the village chief and his counsellors were sitting in a most dignified manner. Everyone was waiting for them to signal the start.

Two tam-tam players were standing on the bank when the chief declared the festivities open. They began to beat their tam-tams rhythmically together. Everyone fell silent as the village chief made a speech which basically said that everyone had to look out for each other. I remember him insisting that the fishing should be joyful, peaceful and good-humoured, as it had been in previous years. A murmur of gratitude rose from the crowd, followed by a huge noise as the villagers threw themselves into the water. The fishermen stood side by side, crouched over, with their harpoons and nets. They then moved forward upriver against the current and caught big fish that wriggled in their hands. They threw them onto the river bank where others collected them.

Among the few people left on the bank were the two tam-tam players and me. When I took my flute out of my pocket and began to blow, they smiled and motioned to me to come and play with them. They must have noticed I had trouble with my eyes because I was walking very slowly. If the sun was too bright, they streamed. Or worse, they irritated me and I rubbed them until they burned.

The musicians welcomed me.

'Hello, my boy, how are you?'

'Fine, thank you.'

'I'm Badjo, and he's Seriba. What's your name?'

'Amadou.'

'You must be the son of the master bricklayer?'

'Yes.'

'My children go to the same school as you. They often talk about a boy who has a problem with his eyes and plays the flute or the harmonica at break. Is that you?'

'Yes, it's me.'

Then they explained that musicians were one big family and that they were very pleased to have me with them.

'Play what you play best and we'll accompany you,' they said.

When I began to play, they followed me on their tam-tams. My lips grew tired of pressing the mouth of my flute for so long. It was the first time I'd played with real musicians. They encouraged me and I gave it my all. We played for about an hour. Then they suggested I had a rest, and they did some real tam-tam drumming. I liked it so much that I began to dance. Over the music, people called out my name to urge me on. And so we livened up the fishing festival as the heat of the afternoon cooled.

People started coming out of the water and assessing their catch, both in terms of quantity and quality. Badjo, Seriba and myself were in for a wonderful surprise. The fishermen divided the catch into three equal piles, and gave one to us. And my two new friends in turn gave me a fish from their share. Later when my friends came out of the water to fetch me and take me home, they were astonished at the amount of fish I had. I had more than they had got by fishing, and a voice inside me said, 'Amadou, your illness prevented you from going into the water. But your music got you more fish.'

When I got home, my mother couldn't believe her eyes. She hugged me tight. My sisters cried with joy. I was very moved, so happy and proud. They all asked me what I had done to get so many fish. I told them about Badjo, Seriba and our musical show. My mother, who knew Badjo's wife, went over to thank them for their generosity on behalf of our whole family. This kind of little courteous gesture is very much part of Malian social custom. She came back with compliments about me from Badjo himself. I'd never heard such praise from anyone. My father also realised something that day. He was very proud of me too and clasped me to him in his big bricklayer's arms. I think that was the day I began to hope I might earn my living as a musician. I didn't take it for granted, however, because that first concert made me realise that I'd have to work very hard to become the professional I dreamed of being. But I was burning with desire and that gave me the strength I needed.

But destiny, which had given me the chance to find my musical self that day, had a dirty trick in store for me. I lost my little brother, Moussa. The day after the fishing festival, we both set off for the creek. We wanted to bathe because it was a very hot day. We weren't afraid of the water because it wasn't very deep, and it was calm. We laughed and played in the sun's reflection. Suddenly I no longer saw or heard my brother. I called to him, at first softly, and then more loudly. I searched for him in the water, in a panic. I finally shouted for help and the whole village came running.

We looked for Moussa in the water for a long time. We eventually found him, but he was dead. He had drowned. Like most Malians, we couldn't swim. Mali doesn't have a coastline. I was very upset by that very brutal death. I kept the sadness of the moment deep inside myself and since that day I developed a real fear of water. I never went bathing again. Much later in my life, when I heard that Ray Charles had had the same unhappy experience, I smiled. I understood that hardship, blindness, that death of a loved one, had shown us both the way through life. But to see this way, we had to accept the obstacles that went with it.

15

After the fishing festival, I was no longer unknown in Douansan. My misfortune limited my activities at school, and with my family and friends, but they seemed to appreciate me more and more. At school now, as well as playing at break, my teacher asked me to play the Malian national anthem at the end of the day. So I became official class musician. Sometimes my teacher even let me sing in class.

My musical success didn't stop my eyes deteriorating, it was no barrier to the pain that had begun to envelop me. My eyes streamed the whole time now. My teacher told me I should see a doctor. I said there was no point because I knew what the problem was. I told him about my cataracts, but he said it didn't seem normal to him that someone rubbed their eyes so much. He thought I should get assessed. He told my father who asked his boss Siri Bankoura for help. 'Boss' Bankoura made an appointment for me with the chief nurse in the training camp. Everyone knew him and called him 'Major' out of respect. He examined me for a long time and asked me a multitude of questions that I answered as best I could. He held my eyes open, shone a light in them and then examined them under his magnifying glass. Then he fixed his eyes on mine so close that I could smell cigarettes on his moustache, and felt his thick beard on my cheeks. He showed me drawings on the blackboard and asked me to describe them. I either didn't see them very well, or I didn't see them at all. I could see, however, that the nurse was a good man. But by the way he shook his head, I understood that he felt very sorry for me.

'How do you manage in class, Amadou?'

'At first I managed to see the letters on the blackboard, but lately my sight has got a lot worse. Now I can only see the teacher's silhouette. I can't read the letters any more. So that I don't get too far behind, my classmate in the next desk helps me by reading what the teacher writes and I copy it into my notebook.'

'Do you have problems reading the letters in your book?'

'No, if I hold it ten centimetres from my eyes.'

'Do you often get headaches?'

'Yes, often. And I can't understand why my eyes water. I'm not sad but I always have tears running from my eyes.'

'It's because the corneas are infected. It's the way your body defends itself against bacteria. Your tears clean the cornea and disinfect it. I'll give your father some medicine to treat your eyes. Now go and sit in the corridor, I want to speak to your father. Good luck.'

'Thank you, Major.'

He said goodbye and, by way of encouragement, patted me on the back. He then took my father into the consulting room. I could hear my father's voice from the corridor, he said only, 'Yes', or 'Good' or 'OK'. I also heard the words 'Bamako' and 'Ophthalmological Institute' several times. They talked for a long time and my father's last words were 'That's settled, then.' He joined me on the veranda, took my hand and led me home. On the way he gave me the gist of what the nurse had said.

'He gave me a bottle of eyedrops for you to use three times a day. If all goes well, we'll move to Bamako in a few months and try to get an operation that could save your eyes. Apparently it's now possible to take out the crystalline lenses and replace them with artificial ones. He said that as well as the cataracts you've had an infection of the corneas for many years. He's very worried about that.'

'But, Papa, what is an infection of the cornea? Did the cataracts do that?'

'I asked that same question and he said no, the two things aren't linked. He said that tomorrow he would write a letter for me to take to the new Ophthalmological Institute. Boss Bankoura is a very nice man, but more than that, he has a lot of influence in our service. He has given me hope that we can save your eyes. I hope you won't lose your sight completely. It will be a bitter pill to swallow if, despite everything, you go blind. Because here in Mali, what can a blind person do but sit in the street and beg? Please God, spare us that!'

When we reached our house, my father went over the whole situation again for my mother and told her we were moving to Bamako. My mother liked the quiet life in Douansan but she agreed in the hope that my sight would be saved. We stayed for a few more months, until the end of the school year, until I learned that I'd gone up into year six. This was June 1966. The first drops of rain were falling and the earth absorbed them eagerly after a six-month drought.

Chapter Three
Seeing

Not long afterwards my father came home with the letter authorising our move to Bamako. It had been granted for family reasons. He announced the big day was imminent and reminded me that we owed it all to Boss Bankoura and the Major who had pleaded our case with the Minister of Social Affairs who, to top it all, had given us a small sum of money for moving costs.

While we waited to leave, my eyes kept on streaming and my anxiety increased. I remember playing some real music but plenty more in my dreams. I could see myself on stage giving concerts, sometimes with my harmonica, sometimes with my flute. My friendship with Seriba and Badjo grew, I visited them nearly every week. I was twelve and they were much older: Badjo only about ten years, but Seriba was almost my father's age. From what my eyes were still able to show me, Seriba was thin and serious. At his house, I always found him doing something other than music, which made me feel uncomfortable. When I went to see Badjo, on the other hand, I could hear him playing as soon as I turned the corner of his street. The sound of his tam-tam resounded as if it were calling to me. As soon I stepped through the door we started playing together, rhythms he composed himself for the main part. When we weren't playing music, we'd talk about it. We'd discuss the role of musicians in Malian society and the lives they lead. He admitted, and I found this really moving, that he couldn't have chosen a better life, that he loved the one he had. And it amazed me to hear him confide in me the power that music had over girls. I loved playing, chatting and laughing with him. I spent many precious moments in his company.

He was much wiser and more experienced than me, of course, and I took advantage of his knowledge. His favourite phrase was, 'A good musician is one who can also play without a score.' And in fact, he improvised rhythms which I then joined in on my flute. He warned me about the future too. He said I would face many obstacles, but I must never be discouraged. 'Only when you've overcome all the difficulties will you be a professional musician, on condition of course that you always play with musicians better than yourself.' I invariable replied that I wanted it so much I was sure I would succeed. We also talked about my eyes. He knew they were the biggest obstacle to my career as a musician. He encouraged me to find a remedy, to have an operation. I told him that was what the Major had told my father and that we were going to Bamako to have it done. He was delighted and laughed as he said that my eyes would help me see the 'pearls' that I would meet later as a professional musician. He was talking about girls, of course!

The days leading up to our departure went slowly. School was closed, the weather was quite cool because the first rains had come. So we had nothing to do but enjoy ourselves as we waited. The end of our life in Douansan would also be the start of our life in Bamako. My mother used to say, 'Everything is beginning and end. The present doesn't actually exist, since our all-encompassing life is itself an uninterrupted transitory stage between the past – the day we were born – and the future – the day we die.'

We didn't leave Douansan on any old day. We left on a Wednesday, because my father thought Wednesday was a propitious day to leave. Like many Malians of his generation, he watched for signs, he listened to superstitions. For him, days weren't all the same, each had its aura, its strength, its special weaknesses. Saturday, for instance, was perfect for pleasure, parties, celebrations. So we didn't leave on a Saturday because our departure wasn't an entirely happy one. The reasons for it, the need to treat my illness, cast a small shadow over our leaving.

On the day itself, my father ordered two donkey-drawn carts to take our baggage to the bus station. We didn't have the means to rent a vehicle to take our belongings all the way to Bamako. I got my flute ready to play on the journey. But at the station, I was so fascinated by the hustle and bustle of the crowd that I forgot about my instrument. My father gave us each a ticket. The driver's assistant loaded the bags onto the roof and covered them with a large tarpaulin tied with a strong rope. I waved goodbye to Seriba and Badjo who had come to see me off. They told jokes to make me laugh. The driver stood at the door of the bus with his list and called passengers one by one. Each said 'Here' before climbing into the bowels of the bus. When all the places were taken, we set off among a tumult of goodbyes, laughing and crying.

The bus drove through the outskirts of Douansan before

taking the main road to Bamako. I tried to engrave the image of the village on my memory, looking out at it one more time. But that image, through the bus window, was very blurred. I could hardly distinguish anything, only the dark silhouettes of the trees lining the two sides of the road, in two continuous lines.

The journey took the best part of a day. I heard some of the passengers say the bus was as slow as a chameleon. By dusk we were approaching Bamako. My sister, who was sitting next to me, asked if I could see the lights of the city. I could only make out a tiny distant luminous spot. When we finally arrived at the main bus station, some of my father's colleagues were waiting in a truck to help us take our baggage to our new house. It had been a long tiring day. But more than anything, it had been frustrating. Everything was new. I needed to discover everything, see everything. But I couldn't see. I couldn't imagine what my brothers and sisters had been oohing and ahhing about all the way. The truck left us in front of our new abode, a modest house, newly built but with no comforts.

The Monday after we arrived in Bamako, my father put the letter from Boss Bankoura and the Major in his pocket, took me by the hand, and we went to the Ophthalmological Institute. My heart was beating so loud my father could hear it. He asked why I was afraid. I told him I was worried about the operation being painful.

'What are you talking about? We're still not even sure you'll be operated on straight away. And, anyway, as far as I know, patients are put to sleep before the operation. You've no reason to be afraid.'

'Is that what anaesthetic means?'

'Yes, it's a medicine that makes you feel nothing, it puts you to sleep artificially.'

'A friend in Douansan told me about his uncle's operation. Apparently the doctors took his two eyes right out of their sockets to operate on, then they put them back again.'

'Ha, ha, ha, you kids tell each other all sorts of tales. I don't believe half of them. I think they can operate without taking eyes out of sockets. Anyway, if it were like that the Major would have warned you. He told me the operation didn't take very long, and he also said you shouldn't have breakfast on the day you go to the Institute in case they want to do blood tests. We'll see. I only hope we won't have to wait too long for the operation.'

'Will I be able to see afterwards, Papa?'

'It's my dearest wish, son, and that of the whole family.'

We got off the bus at the Ophthalmological Institute. Holding my hand, my father walked me for about five minutes before passing through the gate guarded by two sentinels. People who wear uniforms seem to have a natural bond because my father – who'd had military training – and the guards saluted each other. One of them gave us special treatment. With the other visitors he only pointed the way, but he accompanied us to the door of the department and told us to go to the third floor. The first thing we noticed was a strong smell of surgical spirit. There were two ways to get to the third floor: stairs or lift. But my father said there was a notice on the lift saying 'Elderly people, disabled people and sick people only' and a guard was controlling access. My father saluted him too and he ushered us into the lift. It was my first time in a lift, and my tummy went all queasy.

The lift stopped with a jolt and we got out. On an interminable veranda, I could see the silhouettes of people sitting on benches. My father went straight up to a door and knocked. The doctor, a sporty-looking man much older than my father, bid us enter. From what I could make out, white hair stuck out from under his doctor's cap.

Malian courtesy demands that after saying hello and shaking hands, you ask a person how he is, and he usually replies,

'Everything's fine, no problems.'

'And your family, are they well?'

'They're fine too.'

'And is your business doing well?'

'Can't complain.'

Well, with this doctor the conversation was the other way round. He asked all the questions.

'You're Mr Bagayogo, aren't you? The Major phoned to tell me to expect you. What's your son's name?'

'Amadou.'

'My name is Monsieur Bah.'

'Pleased to meet you Doctor Bah. I have a letter for you.'

My father took out the letter Boss Bankoura and the Major had composed and gave it to him. Dr Bah read it very carefully. Then, without more ado, he made me sit on a chair and told me to put my chin on something that held my head still. He said to open my eyes wide, then shone a light into them. I could feel the beam toing and froing over my eyes. He followed that with some drops that stung a bit and said to wait a few minutes. Meanwhile, he asked my father a lot of questions. I was astonished to hear him say so little about my cataracts. All the questions were about the infection that made my eyes stream. By his murmured comments, I understood that he wasn't at all happy with what he saw. He said my eyes needed urgent attention and that the post-operative care meant I would have to stay in hospital so he could follow my progress. He finished this first meeting by saying it was a pity I'd been so long without proper attention.

A little later Dr Bah made me stand on a chair to examine me again. This time he put something round on my eyes that I had to look through. He left the light on so long it became unbearable and I had to tilt my head, I could barely squint or raise my eyelids. I could see even less than before, not even silhouettes, approximate shapes or movements. The doctor then took my hand gently and sat me on a chair.

I heard him tell my father that the best he could hope for was to make sure that I would always be able to see the light of day. He said he would do his utmost but couldn't promise anything. This reassured my father. He added that I didn't have to follow the Major's treatment any longer because the infection had been cured. But it had had side effects and he asked a nurse to take me to the lab for blood, stool and urine tests.

When you can't see, you get used to imagining what is going on. You put a face to each voice you hear. From the pressure of the nurse's hand on mine, I gave him a face and imagined he was tall. I was a little scared so I asked if they were going to operate straight away.

'No, first we need to do some tests. Before operating we need to make sure you have no other illnesses that could debilitate your body.'

'My eyes are my only problem.'

'You don't know that until we get the test results. Sometimes people carry microbes for months, even years, without knowing it. What's your name?'

'Amadou. What's yours?'

'My name is Monsieur Traoré. But everybody calls me just plain Traoré. Careful here, there are some stairs.'

It was obvious Traoré was used to leading blind people. I had no problem climbing the stairs with him. He told me to wait on a metal bench. He came back with the instruments for the tests. While I was away giving these multiple samples, Dr Bah was explaining the situation in more detail to my father. If the results were negative, if I had no other illnesses, he would operate within the week, assisted by two French colleagues Drs Loréal and Jubin. If, however, I didn't get a clean bill of health, I'd have to be treated for that first.

When I came back, he turned to me.

'Amadou, I'll have the test results tomorrow. Your father will come in the afternoon and we'll arrange the day for the operation. Don't be scared, I'll do my best to save your eyes, or at least save what can be saved.'

Dr Bah gave my father some papers and we left.

My father talked a lot on the way home. I sensed he was very affected by what Dr Bah had told him.

'Will I be able to see again?' I asked.

'That's what Dr Bah and I were discussing. You know, Amadou, I'm very worried about your eyes. But you also know that in life things happen for a reason, they're inevitable because they're predestined. Destiny decides what will be, how it will be, when it will be, and human beings have no choice but to accept it. In our family history, no one has ever had eye problems. As far as I remember, one of my father's uncles was paralysed at the end of his life, but no one else has ever had a serious illness. From what Dr Bah told me, it isn't the cataracts that ruined your sight but the infection we didn't treat in time. He called it trachoma, he said it's more dangerous than a cataract.'

That was the first time I'd heard the word. I asked my father if each symptom had a name. He said it did, but that I shouldn't be alarmed.

'You're growing into a man, it's better to face your destiny than waste time feeling sorry for yourself, crying over spilt milk. Every misfortune has its advantages, but we human beings hate misfortune so much that we lose sight of the good things it teaches us. My main worry is for your schooling if your sight can't be saved. There is still no proper infrastructure for teaching blind people in Mali.'

'Does that mean I'll be blind, Papa?'

'We're not sure, but it's a possibility we have to face. Dr Bah said he had saved many people with cataracts but against trachoma he is powerless. Even in developed countries they can't cure it apparently.'

Chapter Four
Eyes Out of Their Sockets

At home, my father gave my mother a run-down of what
had happened at the doctor's. I couldn't see her face very
well but I guessed from her silence and her hand
movements that she was crying. The whole family was sad.
My brothers and sisters crowded round and asked the same
questions I had asked my father.

Since our arrival in Bamako, I hadn't played my flute or
harmonica. But that day I had two options: stay in my room
and cry about the sad fact of becoming blind, or lose myself
in my instruments. I took up my flute and started playing.
My sadness passed. As I played, my room filled with
spectators, my brothers and sisters and neighbours who
obviously found consolation in my melodies. I was no
longer sad, and not exactly happy either. But I'd got used to
drowning my sorrows in music. Now I understood that my
sadness was like a swimming pool in which I could dilute
my misfortune. I kept playing until I heard my mother
calling me to come and eat.

At mealtimes, we boys shared a big plate with my father.
The girls shared another with my mother. We ate with our
hands as my father wished, according to our tradition, so
that we had direct contact with our food. Father argued
against spoons, saying, 'Food should not only go from the
mouth to the stomach, it should be touched by our hands

because our hands have tilled the earth to sow the seeds; when the seeds sprouted, our hands weeded the field to save the young shoots, and when the plants ripened, our hands harvested the grain. It is only natural that those same hands take the food to our mouths. But a tiny part of the first handful should be spilled on the ground to honour our ancestors. Their blessing will make the land fertile and the rains plentiful.'

We children had to heed our traditions. They were imposed on us until we turned fifteen, the age at which boys are circumcised. I was coming to the end of my twelfth year when my parents asked me if I wanted to eat alone. I said yes. In Africa, in large families, this is a sign that a boy is growing up. Parents respect his maturity by according him certain privileges, like eating by himself. I felt honoured. I think they suggested it also because of my eyes. From that day, my mother put my food ration under a little mango tree just beside my room.

One day, when I was eating alone, my mother sat beside me and started talking about her brother, Mamadou Diarra whom we all called Uncle Madou out of respect. He was nicknamed 'Embassy' because he was a chauffeur at the Czechoslovakian Embassy. My mother promised that after my operation we would go together to see Uncle Madou because he had a lot of friends who were professional musicians. She added, 'Since music is so important to you, I'm going to try and bring you some joy as you go through this really difficult time. You're too young to cope with so much anxiety. Your uncle plays the guitar, the flute, the harmonica and even the tam-tam. He has all these instruments in his house and his musician friends play in many bands in Bamako. I can't remember their names but I think they're among the best bands in town.'

This news soothed my soul. It's true, disagreeable things make you ill, but agreeable things encourage you and motivate you to get through bad times. My mother was never really interested in my music but she wasn't displeased when I played my instruments. The promise she just made showed she wanted to make me happy. She wanted to raise my morale before the operation.

'Amadou.'

'Yes, Mother.'

'Every individual has a path he is predestined to walk. A mother is willing to give everything for her child, even part of her own life if she could. But mere humans can't alter the path the Lord God has chosen for a child. Your father and I are here beside you, as we are for your brothers and sisters, and we will be all your life. But there are trials and tribulations that parents cannot shield their children from. You must accept your destiny. The whole family is praying that your operation will be successful and helps you to enjoy your two eyes. But if it is not, it won't be the end of the world. Many people of your age are blind and live the life God lends them here on earth.'

'Mother, I don't want to worry about my operation too much. I'm very grateful that we left Douansan for Bamako. Here I have the opportunity to have this operation. Thank you for that. I shall be even happier if afterwards you take me to see Uncle Madou so I can learn music with his friends.'

'I promised to take care of it. You can be sure I'll keep my promise.'

That conversation was music to my heart and inspired me to write melodies. I understood that my life was to be my muse. A melody came to me and I translated it into music for my flute. The little song went like this:

'Amadou, Amadou!
You'll have your operation
You'll see with your two eyes the light of day
You'll find your own path without the help of anyone
You'll admire the trees, the hills, the rivers
You'll contemplate Bamako and all its wonders
You'll see the sunset behind the mountains
You'll savour life to the full
Amadou, Amadou!
You'll have your operation'

I practised it a bit, and managed to play it. No one would understand its true meaning but me. It had the astonishing effect of preparing me for my operation. I played my flute until the sun went down. After eating, I lay on my bed, satisfied and happy at having found the song 'Amadou, Amadou' for myself. Early the next morning, my father went to see Dr Bah. He came back late in the afternoon with the results of my test in the big pocket of his shirt.

After our meal, he talked to my mother for a long time and then called me.

'Amadou, your test results are satisfactory. Dr Bah laughed and said you're as fit as a five-year-old buffalo, so we set the date for your operation. He's found a bed for you in a room for two people. He said we should occupy it as soon as possible, so we'll go tomorrow. Your operation is the day after. Put some clean clothes in your bag. Don't forget your toothbrush and your plastic sandals.'

My heart started pounding in my chest. Although my father assured me my eyes wouldn't be taken out of their sockets, I wasn't totally convinced. I made a big deal of it. I asked my father again for details of the operation. He laughed, 'Dr Bah was very amused by the eyes-out-of-sockets idea. But remember what he told you about the operation not being very long if there are no complications. Apparently it's the trachoma that has damaged your corneas, it's pointless speculating on the outcome of the operation.'

I went to my room and my mother followed me. We packed the bag I'd be taking to the hospital. My mother asked one of her sisters, who we called Tanti, to come and make food for my father and my brothers and sisters, wash their clothes, sweep our yard, while she was with me in hospital. Tanti came over and my mother spent the rest of the day giving her instructions. I didn't know what to do with the time left until sunset, so I went to bed early so as to be ready for the operation. I slept till the cock crowed. After breakfast, my father helped me on with my bag and I went off down the street between them holding my mother's hand.

When we reached the Institute, Dr Bah was waiting with his two French colleagues. The greeted us and, laughing, said they wouldn't take my eyes completely out of their sockets. The joke made me relax. They then took me to my room. I made out a long figure with white hair who got up from his bed to shake my hand. Dr Bah said, 'Monsieur Bagayogo, allow me to introduce Monsieur Bali Diawarra. I operated on him for mature cataracts last week. He has to stay for a few more days to make sure everything is alright.' I heard my father, my mother and the patient laughing. I didn't understand why Dr Bah's suggestion was so funny. My father added, 'Doctor, you shouldn't have bothered operating on someone who wasn't worth the trouble.' Everybody burst out laughing. The scene is incomprehensible to non-Malians. In Mali, we have a sort of cousinship network, called *sanangougnan* in Bambara, between the clans. They are constantly teasing each other, making fun, and telling funny stories about each other.

This business of blood ties dates back to the Malian Empire which spread over most of West Africa. In order to consolidate friendship and respect between ethnicities, King Soundiata Keïta invented this sort of friendly ribbing and ribaldry. It means ethnic conflicts are rare in Mali. These blood ties exist between the Bagayogo and the Diawarra, between the Keïta and the Doumbia, the Diarra and the Traoré, the Coulibaly and the Keïta, the Samaké and the Keïta. *Sanangougnan* has obligations too. When a Coulibaly or a Doumbia ask a Keïta for a favour, he has to do it. He is forbidden to upset anyone with whom he has this *sanangougnan* relationship. It is very bad luck for anyone to refuse a favour.

The doctor explained to Monsieur Diawarra that I was going to share his room. He said I'd be having my operation tomorrow and my mother would be staying with me. Monsieur Diawarra said he was sorry about my eyes but joked that 'destiny has just offered me a slave to massage my feet.' My mother started making my bed with the sheets she had brought. She organised the room so fast you'd have sworn I'd already been there for months. After Dr Bah had left, Monsieur Diawarra stressed what good hands we were in. He said Doctors Loréal and Jubin were among the best ophthalmological surgeons in Mali. I was very relieved. But I was still anxious about the operation. So Monsieur Diawarra made a suggestion. 'My wife has gone to the market to buy some fruit, but usually she is here with me. I still have four days left in here, my wife and I can look after Amadou. Madame Bagayogo, you can go home with your husband. We'll look after your son. There's no point in you staying too.' My mother politely declined the offer. 'Thank you very much, Monsieur Diawarra, but it would be a nuisance for you. Don't forget you're as much an invalid as Amadou. Why should you take on another burden?'

Monsieur Diawarra insisted so much that my father finally agreed my mother would go with him, and thanked our new friend warmly. When his wife arrived a few hours later with her bag of fruit, the cousinhood jokes started up again. The atmosphere in the hospital room was very jovial. My parents stayed well into the evening. When they came to leave, my father patted me on the shoulder as men do. My mother avoided my gaze so I wouldn't see she was crying.

'God be with you, my child.'

'Thank you, get home safely.'

Chapter Five
In the Dark

When night fell, even the room's big windows didn't give enough light for me to see. I was in the dark. Madame Diawarra advised me to go to bed early to be ready for tomorrow. She heated up some sauce and filled a plate. I washed my hands carefully and ate the food. I said *barka*, which means thank you in Bambara. It is both my native tongue and the official language of the old empire of Mali. These days Bambara is spoken in many West African countries: in Ivory Coast, and in Burkino Faso where it is called Malinké with a slightly different pronunciation for certain words and expressions.

Madame Diawarra gave me some ripe mangoes. When I finished them, she gave me a clean towel and led me to the bathroom. She put some soap in my left hand and placed my right hand on the shower tap. Then she went out and I got undressed. I turned on the tap and water ran over my body. It was a new experience for me. At home we went to the well to get water in a bucket and we didn't need a towel because the sun dried us. We put our clothes straight back on our wet bodies to keep them cool. It sometimes reaches 40 degrees in the shade in Mali. That day I discovered what a shower was, and I savoured it. I found the Institute bathroom much more comfortable than ours.

Back in the bedroom, I thanked Madame Diawarra again

and lay on my bed. I loved her motherly tenderness. I'd often heard my mother say, 'Children belong to everyone, we share them. A mother isn't only a mother to her own children, she's the mother of all children life puts in her way.'

I lay on my bed and dreamed of tomorrow. Normally, I would have taken up my flute to chase away my anxieties. But, there, I could only play in my head. I slept until I felt a cold hand touch my feet gently. It was Madame Diawarra. She led me to the bathroom. After I had washed and had my breakfast, two nurses took me on a trolley to the operating room. There I could make out the white silhouettes of three doctors around a table under a huge lamp. I recognised Dr Bah because of his height and his low voice. They put a sterilised gown on me and disinfected my eyes with a liquid that stung a lot. Dr Bah explained they were going to give me an injection so I wouldn't feel the pain of the operation. I complained my eyes were prickling but he said that was normal, it was the effect of the disinfectant and would soon pass. Dr Bah also said they didn't usually operate on the two eyes at the same time, they did it over an interval of several weeks. But in my case, they had to act quickly. The operation would last an hour because they had to deal with both the cataracts and the trachoma.

'I've already introduced you to my two colleagues and I think you already know Nurse Traoré. We'll do our best to save your eyes. Any questions?'

'Yes, what will happen during the operation?'

'More precisely, the eyes-out-of-sockets question?'

'Yes.'

'Word of honour, that won't happen.'

Even though the white band of their masks covered their mouths, I felt the question that tormented me made them smile. They put a kind of plastic shoes on my feet. Then they tied a tube round my left arm so they could see my veins better. The injection blurred my senses. At times I felt hands press my eyes, and at times I heard male voices.

When I woke, my eyes were bandaged. The voices of my father, my mother and Monsieur and Madame Diawarra were floating around me. They had operated on my cataracts. The first thing that came into my head was to tell my parents how much we had to thank the Diawarras for looking after me as if I were their own child. I don't think I'd really appreciated our Malian customs and traditions until then. But this operation had made me grow up. I had begun to take respect and gratitude very seriously.

Every morning and evening, Dr Bah came to our room to take my bandages off and put an antibiotic ointment on my eyes. Each time he asked if my eyes stung and if I was in pain.

'No, Doctor. My eyes hurt at first but now the pain has passed. When you take off my bandages I feel fresh air over my eyes. I think my skin has become very sensitive.'

'Yes, it's normal. It's because of the bandages, not directly related to the operation. I'm pretty happy with your post-operative condition. It's all coming along nicely. But, as I said before, the trachoma is really the problem. Tomorrow your bandages will come off and we'll have a better idea of what your sight is like.'

'Thank you for everything, Doctor.'

'Best thank God, we rely on His grace.'

The next morning, two nurses came for me. Before we went into the reading room, they took off the bandages and asked if I could follow them without help. I said no.

'Can't you see anything?'

'No.'

'Not even this? Look! How many fingers can you count here?'

'I don't know.'

'Oh my God, Amadou. Not even when I move my hand and fingers like this?'

'When you move your fingers, I feel the air but I don't actually see anything.'

'Let me see your eyes, please.'

He pulled my eyelids up with his thumbs, then said, 'Your scars are almost healed. We have to monitor your sight very carefully. But what you say is worrying. Give me your hand and follow me.'

They took me to a room and sat me in a chair.

'Amadou, you're six metres from a blackboard. Can you see it?'

'Yes, I distinguish it. I know there's something black in front of me.'

They projected big numbers onto the board and asked if I could read them. I couldn't. I only saw a shaft of light. He was so surprised by my reply that he gave a low whistle. He asked me to wait with the other nurse, and we began chatting.

'D'you have a hobby?'

'Yes, music.'

'D'you play an instrument?'

'Yes.'

'Which one?'

'The flute, the harmonica, the tam-tam.'

'You know, Amadou, music is divine. It's not for mere mortals, it belongs to the angels. I know of no worries that a few hours of music can't drown. D'you agree?'

'That's for sure. I want to be a professional musician.'

'That's a good idea. What a beautiful profession you've chosen. Watch out for the "chicks" though. D'you know what "chicks" are?'

'No, but I can guess.'

'Go on, then.'

'Girls.'

'Ha, ha. Right first time. My name is Siné, by the way.'

He took my hand and shook it. I heard footsteps in the corridor. It was Dr Bah and the nurse who had done the eye tests. He was so worried that he had gone off to find the three doctors and Nurse Traoré.

'So, Amadou, how are you feeling?'

'Very well, thank you. And you?'

'Not very well. It appears you failed the tests. You didn't even pass the first stage.'

'No.'

'Our only hope is the cornea transplant, then. But they can only be done in a developed country.'

I could sense the concern of everybody in the room. Dr Bah turned on the light. He projected a beam on the board again and moved it around.

'Do you notice anything?'

'Yes, there's a light moving from left to right.'

'Can you tell me what colour it is? Yellow, red, green…?'

'I can't tell.'

Dr Bah switched off the light and talked about my future.

'Amadou, I said we'd do our best to save your eyes. We took out your two crystalline lenses and replaced them with artificial plastic ones. But before and during the operation we could see your two corneas were damaged by the infection you've had for many years. In some developed countries, ophthalmologists have the means to transplant corneas. But we don't have access to those techniques here yet. That may change if the political situation remains stable. It's not that long ago that people would have thought it impossible that we'd be operating on cataracts here in Mali. The President has said he is committed to fighting illiteracy and disease, and has promised doctors government support. You're still young, so God willing, things will change and you'll benefit from these changes. I'll prepare a certificate saying your sight is clearly below the minimum. Officially we call it a Blind Person's Certificate but I don't like using that word because it makes the holder uncomfortable. We'll give you an ointment to put on your eyes every day. Throw it away after six weeks because it will be infected with microbes. I'll write a report to my colleague, the senior nurse in Douansan, who has kindly asked to know the outcome of your operation. Tomorrow morning, I'll ask your father to come and get you. You'll be ready to leave tomorrow evening. Your scars have healed so there's no point you staying any longer. I'll discuss your future with your father and tell him what I think will be the best for your career. Goodbye, my boy, and good luck.'

They all shook my hand warmly. But I wanted to cry warm tears. Siné said something to make me laugh.

'Hey, James Brown, when you're famous and giving concerts, I hope you'll do me the honour of giving me a seat in the front row. Can I count on you?'

'Yes, you can count on me.'

Dr Bah joined in.

'And what about me, Amadou?'

'Yes, you'll all be guests of honour.'

'OK, we'll hold you to your promise. Goodbye, Amadou. Siné will take you back to your room.'

'Goodbye, Doctor. And thank you for everything.'

'Don't mention it, my son, I know you're going to make it.'

Siné took me back to my room. He said goodbye and also wished me good luck. I told Monsieur and Madame Diawarra about what the future held for me. Monsieur Diawarra said, 'God will lead you by the hand, son. Something good comes of everything. Who knows what grand design God has in store for you? I recommend you believe in God. It will help you accept your life on this earth. Everything that happens is a message from God. We must open our ears and listen to them. I will pray for you, son. The nurse told me you'll be going home tomorrow. That is earlier than we thought. But it stands to reason a child's scars heal more quickly than an old man's. I'll tease my slave, your father, about it. Didn't you know that the Bagayogos are the personal property of the Diawarras? Ha, ha, ha!'

41

All three of us laughed even though the situation was far from cheerful. They were all trying to prepare me psychologically to face my new life, a life in which I would feel everything, hear everything, but see nothing.

My father and mother came to fetch me. Monsieur and Madame Diawarra teased them again. Busily joking, they hadn't time to talk about my eyes. I think it was their way of chasing away their pain. But mine would not go away. I'd been warned I might become totally blind because of the cataracts or trachoma. But I'd always kept hoping that one day, thanks to the advances in surgery, I would see. Now the idea that all medical solutions had been exhausted upset me very much, my hope had died.

My mother began collecting my stuff. I don't know how many times my father thanked the Diawarras. They replied over and over again, 'Don't mention it, Monsieur Bagayogo, Amadou is our son too.'

On the way home, my mother took my hand and said she'd been to see her brother. He had agreed to help me learn the guitar. She added:

'Amadou, we don't lose everything all at the same time. When we lose one faculty, we develop another in a very special way.'

All these words pronounced by one or another of my family and friends prepared me gently for my destiny.

Chapter Six
The Light of Music

After my stay in hospital, I began to see things differently. Whenever I was told a story, it took shape in my imagination. I saw things very clearly in my mind. I gave them colours, places, shapes. I used my ears a lot, sounds came to me more intensely. People often told me I was blessed with an excellent memory and great powers of imagination. I was proud of that.

My sisters welcomed me back home but no one asked me about the operation. I went to my room to change, and took up my flute. I played 'Amadou, Amadou' several times. Then my mother came in. I knew it was her from the fragrance of incense she gave off. She sat on my bed and asked if I was ready to go and see Uncle Madou. I said I'd like to go tomorrow, as soon as possible. We agreed to go in the afternoon, after my uncle finished work at the Czech embassy.

The next day, my father went to get my certificate. It stated my vision was under 0.2 dioptre. No two ways about it, I was blind. My father only showed the paper to my mother and me, as if he didn't want to dwell on my disability but turn the page as quickly as possible. In the late afternoon, my mother came to my room where I was playing my flute. She chose a shirt and trousers for me, saying they matched and I'd look very handsome in them.

Choosing my clothes and dressing was something I'd been able to do myself not that many months ago.

We took the *sotrama*, a minibus, to Uncle Madou's house. He had his big guitar ready. Tanti offered us food and drink. Mother told them of Dr Bah's diagnosis and explained the damage the trachoma had done. Uncle Madou exclaimed, 'Who cares if your operation wasn't a success, Amadou. We're going to make you a big star, the whole of Mali will be proud of you.' And Tanti added, 'We really do hope so. May God hear and help you and may our ancestors ask God to give Amadou strength.' Thirty years later, God answered that prayer.

Uncle 'Embassy' Madou knew from my mother that I loved the flute and the harmonica, but he thought I needed to learn the guitar. He said that one day I was bound to play in a band or even form my own.

He really reassured me and gave me new hope. He convinced me I wouldn't be one of those blind people sitting at home in a corner doing nothing, or those beggars that hang around the main squares of Bamako. Music would be my passage out of poverty. Embassy put my hand on the guitar and asked me to get some sound out of it. We stayed there until night fell. Uncle Madou served the Malian tea you drink three times. You put water in a pot on a little charcoal stove, and when the water boils with the tea, you put sugar and a few leaves of mint in it. Then you serve it in little glasses, usually half full. After you drink the first glass, you refill the pot for the second glass, then the third.

Music-lovers in Bamako have made this ritual extremely pleasurable by making each glass different. The first has a strong bitter taste, the second is less bitter, and the third is nice and sugary. They tease the girls by saying, 'The first glass is bitter like the life that only men face, the second is sweeter like the love that only women have in their heads, and the third is really sweet like children.' Girls usually react by saying, 'Your tongues are too ruined by cigarettes and alcohol to taste the difference.'

Madou laughed and said, 'Just as a car needs petrol to run, I need Malian tea and a cigarette to keep going.'

At the end of the evening, he took us home in the embassy car. I was happy because we'd got along really well. When I got out, he arranged to see me the following week. He wanted to introduce me to other members of his group and have me play the flute and harmonica for them. Then he asked if I played any other instrument. I said I fooled around on the tam-tam but for the audition I preferred to play an instrument I was really good at. He replied, 'I've told them about you, kid. They've a few ideas about things you could do together. Always remember you have real musical talent, even if you don't believe it yourself.'

'Uncle, I don't even know the notes on the guitar.'

'It's not important. Lots of great musicians can't read music. Me too, I played the guitar without a clue what doh, ray, me, fah, soh, lah, te meant.'

'Are they the notes on the guitar, uncle?'

'Yes, the guitar and other instruments. When you play the flute, you obviously play those notes without realising it. The guitar makes those notes too.'

It was 1967. The pain of the failure of my operation began to fade as my mind filled with projects and plans. Ambition was starting to blossom in me.

One Saturday afternoon, my uncle came to fetch me. We drank Malian tea and smoked a few cigarettes. My uncle teased me, as he showed me the packet of 'Freedom' cigarettes made by Sonatam (the Malian National Tobacco and Match Company), saying, 'We have to smoke Made in Mali.' He put the guitar round my neck and said it was acoustic, adding that he had an electric guitar but it was best I begin with an acoustic. He explained what he was going to do with me that day.

'I'm going to introduce you to some great Malian musicians. First we'll go and see Kanté Manfila, he's originally from Guinea and one of the best guitarists in the country. Then we'll go to Tidiani Koné, a great saxophonist who also plays the guitar, the *n'goni* traditional Malian guitar and the trumpet.'

There were three people at Kanté Manfila's house: our host, Tidiani Koné and another man who was preparing tea. The two musicians were already playing. Uncle Madou introduced me as the 'new boy on the Malian scene'. Unlike Kanté, Tidiani was interested in the story of my cataracts. When I finished telling of my misfortune, he said, 'Your uncle has told us about your talent. We'll make one of Mali's finest musicians out of you, you can be sure of that.' I could have cried with joy. I told them that music was my vocation and a way of overcoming my disability. Tidiani asked me if I could sing.

'Yes, a bit.'

'Do you know any Cuban songs?'

'Yes, I've sung a few.'

'Which ones?'

'"El Manisero" and "Guantanamera".'

Kanté started playing the guitar and my uncle took up the bass guitar. Tidiani joined in on the sax and I sang. But I wasn't happy with the way I sang. Sometimes I went too fast, I was concentrating on the tone of the notes. I tried to make my voice sing sharps and then I lost the rhythm. My uncle used a pause in our playing to explain that the rhythm was more important than the actual sound of my voice. He added, 'You have a very beautiful voice, Amadou, but if you force it, it won't last very long. Concerts go on for two to three hours. You won't be able to stretch your vocal chords that long. I'll keep time with my right foot and you try to follow. Listen... pah, pah, pah.'

My uncle began tapping his foot. I followed him and this time I managed to follow the rhythm. Then Kanté played a new tune and asked me to join in on my flute. I didn't manage to do it as he wanted. Then I played 'Amadou, Amadou'. They understood its meaning. Kanté liked it and asked me to sing the words. We had drunk tea and Kanté urged me to hurry since we hadn't much time before dusk, and we still had to get our instruments up on stage and rehearse what we'd done. It was the weekend, people liked going out. Kanté said the concert was sold out. What? We were giving a concert that very night? I exploded with joy. I could have cried. God was giving me a priceless gift, one that gave my life meaning. I didn't have to sit on a school bench any more. I would never have to beg at a crossroads.

I had already learned a bit about patience. I had accepted I was blind. I was no longer ashamed when people led me to the toilet when I needed it. I realised it didn't bother other people at all, they seemed pleased to help.

When we arrived at the place where the concert was to be held, they made me get out of the car first and sit on a chair in the hallway. Kanté tuned a guitar, handed it to me and told me to play something. 'We have to finish setting up the instruments. Try picking out some songs, you'll hear your mistakes as you go along and remember that you only become a weaver by weaving.' He showed me how to hold the guitar.

'Each individual has his own way of holding his guitar but experience has shown me that this way is the least tiring. Later on, when you have to stand for a whole concert, the way you hold your guitar will make all the difference, you'll stand the pace longer.'

Then my uncle gave me a horizontal flute. I'd never seen one like that before, I played the penny whistle type, known as the African flute. Kanté put my fingers on the holes and I got two or three sounds out of it. When the heat of the day started to cool, we went backstage to our dressing room. Kanté introduced the other musicians. Some only played with this band, others played in other bands as well. There was Bah Sotigui Kouyaté (literally 'Bah who has a horse'). Bah played both the alto and soprano sax in the National Orchestra A. There was also Amadou Traoré, nicknamed 'Addès'. He helped me a lot with my singing. And finally there was Zani Diabaté, who played with the National Ballet Orchestra but who wanted to form a band.

For each voice, I created an image. I imagined them all, no doubt differently from what they really were. They all made me feel very welcome. In the dressing room, there were also some girls. Kanté whispered, 'Amadou, we'll only teach you the music, for other things, girls for example, you'll have to manage by yourself. You'll learn, it's only natural. Girls are important because they're musicians' foils, their sounding boards. They're wherever we are, and we're wherever they are. Musicians are the same the world over. In the hereafter, we'll try to get the girls judged with us, won't we?' The others heard this advice and sniggered. The room was full to bursting and very smoky. I didn't care, I was so happy to be there, giving a concert with musicians who had welcomed me so warmly. I was so grateful for the opportunity.

I tried to concentrate and remember all Embassy's and Kanté's advice. If I hadn't been blind, I'd have written it down to remember it. But as it was, I had only my memory to fall back on. I had to develop it twice over to even up my disability. I had a much better memory than most sighted people. A musician who came out of the concert hall announced, 'Hey, guys, I think God's a fan of ours, judging by the numbers who have come to hear us. The hall's as packed full as a new box of matches.' My uncle asked, 'Are you sure they've come to hear you? Perhaps it's for the Rail Band. You're just borrowing their fame.' Tidiani retorted, 'I think we've got new fans. What's more, some ex-Rail Band musicians had a row over some chicks in front of their fans.' They laughed and started gossiping about girls. Kanté brought us back to order by saying we had ten minutes before we were on stage. He told me I'd be singing 'El Manisero', the song we had rehearsed that afternoon. I was to wait in the dressing room until then. He advised me to think over the advice they'd given me.

'Are you nervous?'

'I think so, but since I can't see any faces, probably not as much as all that.'

Someone came into the room. He said, 'Good evening, Amadou. I'm Soungalo Sanogho, alias "The Bear". Are you a musician?'

'I'd like to be.'

'What instruments do you play?'

'The flute, the harmonica and a bit of tam-tam. Tonight I'm going to sing for the very first time in my life with professional musicians like Kanté Manfila and Tidiani Koné. I'd like to learn the guitar, God willing.'

'Zani Diabaté and Amadou "Addès" Traoré are super talented, they can teach you lots about the guitar and singing.'

'I can certainly give you a hand with your singing, if you like,' said Addès.

'Of course I like, Addès, thanks a lot. I accept with pleasure. My uncle works during the week, so I can't play music with him. And I don't go to school any more. I've just had my eyes operated on but it didn't work. I used to see a little bit but now I'm blind. Music is really my passion so I'm grateful to anyone who can help me in some way or other.'

'Don't worry, God helps us all. Your uncle, Kanté and Tidiani are all close friends of mine. We all help each other when needs be. I'll be happy to help you. Where do you live?'

'With my parents, in Bagadadji. I'm going to be spending weekends with Uncle Madou, I'm very happy.'

'Do you sing your own songs or covers?'

'I sing covers most of the time, but I can sing my own.'

'That's useful for me to know.'

'Hey, we're on stage. Our audience awaits,' said The Bear.

'I'll stay with Amadou for a bit, I'll see you in the break, have a good concert,' said Zani.

'Me too, I'll stay with you,' added Addès.

So, Zani and Addès stayed with me. We talked for a long time about my illness and also about music. They described the long road a professional musician must walk and the effort you have to put in to master the guitar.

Chapter Seven
On Stage

When the band started playing, all my organs started vibrating. I felt the sounds and rhythms right down in the marrow of my bones. I smiled when Zani suggested we mingle with the audience. Zani and Addès took my hand and led me into the hall. As we passed through the crowd, I heard people saying hello to my two new friends, well known musicians, and asking who I was. By the volume, I knew we were now near the stage. They made me sit between them and started giving me a few musical tips, like how pieces are composed, the chorus or the scales. They finished by saying it was only a matter of time before I learned the laws governing music.

The band played until the interval. My uncle, Kanté, Tidiani and the others went back to the dressing room. Zani, Addès and I stayed in the hall. Unlike most of his colleagues, Zani hated the smell of cigarettes. Some girls came up and offered us a drink and asked Zani about me.

'He's Amadou, Mali's new rising star. We're preparing him to take over from us. And we've warned him about you chicks.'

'Hey, get off our backs. We offer you a drink and you shame us by refusing one. And worse still, you slag us off in front of Amadou. Is that what they call star arrogance?'

We talked to the girls, who were very nice. The youngest

sat beside me and we chatted. She asked me about my future. I explained that first of all I had to master my instrument.

'One of my friends was with you in the dressing room before the concert. Apparently you sing really well. Are you going to get up on stage tonight?'

'Yes, but I don't know if you'd call me a good singer. If you stay until the end, you'll probably see me up on stage.'

Zani came up and interrupted our conversation, to the girl's annoyance. He called my uncle.

'Embassy!'

'Yes, Zani.'

'What are we doing after the concert?'

'I'm going home with my wife. Amadou is staying at my house for the weekend. During the week, he'll be at his mother's, she's my sister.'

'Well, I suggest taking him home with me to teach him some basics of the guitar and Addès can give him some singing lessons. I really like Amadou. We've got good vibes.'

'Zani, we all belong to the great family of musicians. Amadou is our child. I think he's very talented so when my sister asked me to introduce him to the world of music, I accepted with pleasure. Besides, when he's a star, he'll tell everyone about me! But joking apart, it's better for him to be making music than staying at home bored.'

It was a bit like I was the sacrificial goat whose fate was being decided. When they finished talking, Zani asked me if I was happy about going to his house. I said yes. One of the girls wanted to wriggle her way into the next day's rehearsal but Zani said no, on the pretext that it upset his concentration. Instead, he suggested she came afterwards for Malian tea. So there we were talking, Zani, Addès, three girls and me, when the noise of chairs moving told me that the interval was over. The band had played two or three pieces when Kanté took the microphone and told the audience:

'Ladies and gentlemen, we're honoured and fortunate to have among us a rising star of Malian music, Monsieur Amadou Bagayogo. Take a good look at this face and remember his name. You're the lucky people who one day will be able to say you saw him when he was just starting out. So here's Amadou Bagayogo to sing "El Manisero" by Laba Sosseh. Let's give him a big hand.'

Addès took my hand and led me on stage. Some people whistled, others shuffled in their chairs. My uncle whispered in my ear that he was happy and proud, and all I had to do was remember the advice they'd given me:

'Don't be nervous, concentrate on the rhythm. The drums will give you the beat. OK? Go on then, good luck. Ready? You're on.'

The band began playing 'El Manisero' and I joined my voice to it. The audience was moving about so much that I could feel the vibration up on stage. In my head I heard my uncle's advice about the importance of the rhythm. In the end, it turned out to be the best I'd ever sung. I heard girls' voices crying 'Amadou! Amadou!' That helped my confidence. When the band started playing more softly, I also lowered my voice until it faded away. It was then I heard people shouting 'Encore! Encore! Encore!' My uncle moved over to tell me, 'Amadou, don't move an inch, you're carrying on. It was superb, my boy.' Kanté heard my uncle, and added, 'Your debut is devilish, everything's perfect. Bravo! When you've got it, you've got it. Age doesn't matter. Off you go, let's do it again.'

The band started up 'El Manisero' again, and my voice went with it. This time, it occurred to me to call to the audience now and again. I shouted, 'Is this OK?' They responded with a huge 'Yes!' This time at the end I took a big goodbye bow. Zani and Addès led me off the stage to a deluge of applause, and my name shouted among it.

Back in the dressing room, Zani, Addès and I descended into an eloquent silence. Then Zani said, 'Amadou, I think music will avenge the trick life has played on you. You couldn't see it, but people were so moved by your voice that they were crying. It was very touching. We're going to work on your voice together, it will get even better. But I think you already have a very beautiful voice.'

Then I heard a lot of people moving about in the dressing room. Kanté had tried to stop them because it was too hot and the room too small for them all to fit in. My uncle sat down next to me and confirmed what Zani had said. He described the audience crying with emotion, and he repeated how proud he was of me, and how urgent it was that I got on with learning the guitar. The vote was unanimous that night. They all congratulated me and talked about how moved the crowd had been. Then a female voice broke in.

'Amadou, do you recognise my voice? It's Kadiatou, they call me Kadett. We were talking before the show. D'you remember?'

'Of course.'

'I'll come to see you at Zani's house tomorrow.'

'OK, we'll expect you.'

'See you tomorrow, then.'

'Goodbye, Kadett.'

We stayed in the little dressing room for about two hours with some fans. Then the band was invited to a restaurant where we dined copiously. Zani and Addès were in permanent attendance. They took my hand and helped me walk. It had been agreed I'd spend the night at Zani's house. Before he left, my uncle came and hugged me.

'I'll come and see you tomorrow afternoon.'

'Seriously, Uncle, thanks for everything.'

'Thanks for what, Amadou? Your career is only just starting, I hope we'll go a long way together.'

Zani took my hand and we went off to look for a taxi. He usually got around on a moped, but he explained that he'd left it at home because so many got stolen at the weekend. A car pulled up beside us and the man inside started talking to us.

'Good evening. Is it really you, Zani Diabaté?'

'Yes, it's me, how are you doing?'

'Well, thanks. I'm a fan of yours.'

'Thanks very much, I'm delighted.'

'Can I offer you a lift?'

'If you have the time, thanks.'

'Please get in.'

In the car, Zani and the driver Adama Sy, nicknamed 'Nostradamus', fell into conversation. He sold cloth in Dibida market. He talked about his passion for Kung Fu films and, when Zani gave him his address, La Cité des Infirmiers in Quinzambougou, he exclaimed, 'I'd go crazy if I lived there! How do you survive? There are beautiful women on every corner, it's as if the seed of beauty has been planted there. I wouldn't be able to stop myself wanting to change women every day like I change shirts! My life is karate, women and football.' Before he finally dropped us off, he had talked about all kinds of things and even after we'd got out of the car, he kept on talking to us. Zani was astonished. 'How can a human being talk so much without stopping for breath, like a waterfall? Not a full stop, nor even a comma.' We laughed and made fun of Nostradamus. In the house, Zani began making up my bed, a sofa bed that he pulled out. Then he helped me to the toilet.

When I finally lay down, I couldn't go to sleep straight away. My head was spinning. The evening had been exceptional. The names of all the people I was grateful to went round and round in my head: my mother, Uncle Madou, Kanté Manfila, Tidiani Koné, Addès, Zani Diabaté, Seriba and Badjo in Douansan. I no longer doubted my future as a musician because now I'd made my debut. I was convinced that I was in the right place, among the best musicians in Mali. I went to sleep very late that night, I was so excited imagining my future, and going over the concert again and again in my head.

I awoke to the smell of coffee. Zani had made breakfast and prepared a bucket of warm water for me to wash in. He said he had dreamed of Nostradamus, and had nicknamed him

'Tape Recorder'. He asked me if I had dreamed about him too. I said no, I had spent the night reliving the concert and I was so grateful to all of them.

We started our guitar lesson straight away. He made me play the scales, taught me the notes. Then, he linked the notes to numbers: doh = 1, ray = 2, me = 3, fah = 4, etc. He played them on the guitar and said I should do the same. I managed three of them. We then went on to the combinations. The exercise was hard for me, because since I couldn't see the notes, I had to tackle them differently, find my own method of recognising them.

We worked for an hour before I succeeded in playing the combination of notes Zani was teaching me. Then he took me into the courtyard of his house and told me to wait under the mango tree while he went off to do a moped training course. I played for a long time. Two girls joined me. One asked if I could play the guitar. I identified her as one of Kadett's friends. She said she was, and that Kadett was coming. She asked if I wanted something to eat or drink while we waited. 'My name's Rokia Koumaré, people call me Rose. And my friend is Djénèba Traoré, she's called Janine.' We stayed there talking until Zani came back.

I practised hard that day. It gave me a lot of real satisfaction. When it was time to take a break, I didn't want to put the guitar down. I held it in my arms like something I cherished. Zani made fun of me. Then he talked to me about Kadett.

'You have to wait for her this afternoon. Do you remember her?'

'Of course I do. How could I forget her? I only met her last night. But I thought she was coming to see you…'

'No, the ones who came to see me are already here. Poor old Amadou, all this at once. Well, my boy, things are happening like wildfire for you.'

'Zani, I'm delighted that things are changing fast, otherwise I'd be at home bored or miserable.'

'I can't disagree. But the Good Lord never gives everything altogether nor takes it all away. That's life. Remember what James Brown says in one of his songs: "It's life and everything is possible." He's one of the greats, James Brown.'

'Yes, I love his music, but I'm better at singing Cuban music. My knowledge of English is zero.'

'That's normal. We're in a French-speaking country. English isn't very popular here. I almost asked a friend who plays the double bass to help me learn English. He wants to play in my new band. If you want, I'll ask him to teach you the basics too. English is a very important language. All professional musicians speak it fluently.'

'I know two words in English, *yes* and *no!*'

From the intensity of the sun, I could tell it was nearly noon. We moved under the veranda. Rose and Janine would soon be coming to serve us some food. I thought of the girls and wondered which one was interested in Zani. But it wasn't appropriate to ask the question. In Malian tradition, since Zani was a friend of my uncle's, the same generation, I couldn't commit such an indiscretion. I couldn't be the one to bring up the subject of women. Zani pushed the furniture back to make room for a plastic tablecloth. We sat round a big plate. We ate with our hands and no one spoke, as is the custom. We have to respect our food because it is a gift from God that not everybody has. Also, respecting your meal is respecting yourself: a person is what he eats. At the end of the meal, I said *barka* for the food, and to Rose and Janine I said *Aw ni goua*, which means literally 'It's very good'.

The time for Malian tea had arrived. Rose unpacked the pot, the glasses and lit her little charcoal stove. We all sat round it. Zani picked up his guitar and sang some classic Cuban songs like 'El Manisero,' 'El Varadero', and 'Guantanamera'. I still went too quickly at times and Zani interrupted me and got me back in time and asked me to tap out the beat with my foot. It worked and our singing sounded very good to our ears. So much so that Rose and Janine got up and danced. According to Zani, I had the advantage of not having complexes, and that was a trump card in a musician's pack. I replied that it was one of the few privileges blind people had. It was true, I couldn't be afraid of looks I couldn't see. Not being able to see other people, freed me from a burden that sighted musicians carried.

We interrupted the session when I thought I heard my uncle's car. But Zani whispered in my ear that in fact it was our friend from the previous night, Tape Recorder. He sat with us and began his verbal diarrhoea. Zani tried to shut him up by playing the guitar but Nostradamus wouldn't let him. He said in a very serious tone that he had a business proposition and needed to see us in private.

He got his wish, and he, Zani and myself went into the sitting room. He went round in circles until Zani asked him to get to the point of why he had come. He explained, 'I've been thinking a lot about Amadou since last night. I want to help him get his sight back. I think his eyes could be saved.'

'By an operation?'

'No, not by modern medicine. I know a witch doctor who cures blindness just by the force of the Koran. He possesses a secret that enables him to do it, don't ask me how. Like most people I think there are many things human eyes can't see and human hands can't feel. It's sad that such a young man…'

'I don't mean to interrupt you, Nostradamus, but do you personally know anyone who has got their sight back thanks to this magician? And if you do, how much does it cost?'

'Yes, of course I know someone who has personally benefited from his help. Otherwise I wouldn't have come to see you. Haven't you ever heard of this kind of phenomenon?'

'Yes, but don't forget we're in Bamako, a town where rumours abound, a town where we have to take all we hear with a pinch of salt. Listen, Nostradamus, it's obviously not up to me to decide. Amadou is the son of the sister of a musician friend who is arriving at any moment. All the same, I can tell you frankly that if it was up to me, I'd say no.'

'Why's that?'

'Because I'm very cautious. How much does he ask for this service?'

'A few months ago, he opened an eye for a hundred thousand Malian francs. He began with one eye, and if the patient was satisfied, he did the other.'

'And have you talked to people he has cured?'

'Yes, my own aunt. I can introduce you to her.'

'Was she really blind?'

'Yes, she could only get around with a stick. And I've known other people the healer has helped. I think they should talk about it on the radio. But I don't know if he would agree because he doesn't like too much publicity.'

'What's his name?'

'El Hadji Almadoun Maïga. He's from the north of Mali.'

'Let's wait for Embassy, Amadou's uncle.'

Chapter Eight
Stories True and False

I had understood Zani was sceptical. Personally, I didn't really know what to think. Ever since the doctors had said I couldn't even count the fingers on a hand in front of my nose, I'd lost all hope of seeing the light of day again. I had begun to get used to this new state of affairs, and accept my destiny. I was resigned to using all my senses except my sight.

Tape Recorder hadn't made a very good impression on us anyway. He talked too much to be taken seriously. But I still thought we should try everything because I had nothing to lose. When my uncle arrived, Zani mostly spoke about my prowess on the guitar. Then he brought up what Nostradamus had said. Uncle Madou asked Nostradamus a lot of questions, and the latter stressed the case of his aunt. I felt my uncle was persuaded. Before leaving, he gave us his spiel again. 'My only motivation is the pity I feel for Amadou. I have young brothers his age at home. I'd be delighted to help him. My aunt who couldn't see at all, now has brilliant eyes, amazing eyes, eagle eyes.' We made an appointment with him for the following day to discuss it again.

After he'd left, we talked about him. Zani told my uncle how we had met. Embassy made his position clear. 'I've heard about these things before, but I'm not totally convinced.' Zani was eager to know what my parents would think about it. My uncle laughed because he was sure my mother would want to see the shaman right away. While we were getting ready to go and see my parents, Kadett and Addès arrived. They came with a friend who wanted to meet me, Salimata Coulibaly, known as Sylvie. I explained we were very sorry but we had to leave. They teased me, asking if I'd learned such gentlemanly behaviour from Zani. When Addès heard why we weren't keeping our appointment, he was very cynical. He thought it ridiculous we were even bothering to talk to my parents about it. He said we should call the police to arrest these crooks instead, that these practices were serious in the eyes of Islam and that these were the kind of fanatics you got in Christianity. He cited the example of the Pope who forbade the use of condoms. These fanatics weren't in tune with reality and modernity. He was sure that if we gave them money, we'd never see it again. Addès went ranting on like that for quite some time. He was a philosopher, and to make us understand his point, he told us a story.

'You all know the madman that children and young girls like making fun of and getting to dance? A very beautiful tall black guy with scars on his face showing his origin, he's from a village on the border of Mali and Burkina Faso. Well, listen to his story. He was a merchant, selling cloth. He was happy because his business was going well. He had several houses that he rented out and his family was proud of him. One day, in his neighbourhood, a shaman he knew with a reputation for being very serious, came to him with a proposition: he knew how to make him rich. To gain his confidence, the shaman showed him a suitcase full of Malian notes. He told him to grab a handful and buy whatever he wanted so he could see the money wasn't fake. When the man was convinced, the shaman told him to bring six million Malian francs and he promised to double it. But the madman, whose name is "Double" by the way, didn't have that kind of money. So he sold his houses and his shop, thinking he was going to make a fortune. His wife disapproved but he took no notice. When Double brought him the money, the shaman told him the date on which spirits would put his profit in a new suitcase on the bank of the Niger River. On the day in question, he was there for the rendezvous but the suitcase wasn't. He went mad, he started repeating over and over again, "I've a right to double! I've a right to double!" As you can imagine, the shaman was nowhere to be seen.'

We were all amazed at the man's huge naivety, but Addès said, 'We're always wise after the event.'

A little later, we found my father sitting under a tree in our yard and my mother busy at the oven. We drank some fresh water and Zani began by saying how wonderful I was. My father thanked Zani formally. He had heard him on Radio Mali. Zani said how glad he was to have met me and how much he liked me. My father said his piece:

'His mother and I thank you very much for what you're doing for him. We are very sad that he can't have the second operation and he'll never have all his visual faculties. At present, there is nowhere for young blind people to learn

Braille and continue their schooling. When Dr Bah gave me his Blind Certificate I went to the Ministry of Education to find out what was available. They are thinking of creating a school where young blind people can keep studying but it's not a priority right now. They're attending to more urgent problems. We've been independent for too short a time to be worrying about blind people. We're just starting to build.'

Embassy finally related the discussion with Nostradamus as precisely as he could. He didn't forget to say that most of us were pretty dubious about the whole thing. He suggested he and Zani pay for it but he needed their consent. My father seemed very suspicious, he didn't take the thing very seriously. He asked my mother, who thought anything was worth a try. She believed certain people have supernatural powers. She wanted to meet Tape Recorder's aunt to verify the shaman's talents. We went on to discuss the supernatural, things we couldn't understand, the impalpable. Everyone told some story or other that he had heard about people whose illness had been cured by these 'traditional doctors'. In some cases, it was possible to find rational explanations for these sudden miracles. My father, Ibrahima, ended by saying that he would be convinced when he had proof, after he saw Tape Recorder's aunt, 'Let's wait to see her eagle eyes, her brilliant eyes, before we make up our minds.'

We finally drove back to Zani's in my uncle's car. All the girls had disappeared except Rose. She prepared a salad and served it. I played a bit more with Zani then Addès gave me a few singing tips.

'We usually start singing on 1. For example, on songs with four beats, we count: 1 - 2 - 3 – 4. 1 - 2 - 3 - 4. If you sing "taaa! tooo! taaa! taaa!" your first "taaa" must be on the 1. You can also go on the half beat, for instance 1, taaa, 2, tooo, 3, taaa, and so on. D'you understand? Another thing, don't force your voice if you can help it. You can raise or lower it but don't force it, OK?'

Shortly after, Addès complimented me, he said I learned very quickly. But now I had to go home. Zani and Rose wanted me to stay, but I wanted to be alone in my room to practise the guitar.

I arrived home on the pillion of my uncle's motorbike, an acoustic guitar slung across my back. In fact, I didn't play when I got back, but discussed the weekend with my parents. They'd got wind of my exploits at the concert, and the audience's emotional response. I proudly showed them the money my uncle had given me in payment. My father was very happy.

'The Good Lord knows how to do things. You had to suffer before you found your way. Music is obviously your thing.'

'Yes, father, it's true. I love it, and I noticed last night that through music you receive a lot of human warmth. The audience listens to you, and admires you. It gives you a lot of satisfaction.'

I spent the next day practising. In the late afternoon, Zani and Addès came to take me to see Nostradamus. Around five o'clock, we were comfortably installed at Zani's in the armchairs under the mango tree. An hour later, with reassuring punctuality, Tape Recorder was there. He hadn't even got through the door when he started talking. Zani remarked on his 'soldier's punctuality', and this set him off on a long speech.

'Oh no, don't compare me with soldiers. You know the jokes people tell about them. "I can do nothing, I know nothing, give me a military uniform and put a gun on my shoulder."'

Nostra was alone, so Zani asked him where his aunt was. He explained she hadn't been able to come today because she was very busy and hadn't had time to get organised. He said that now she could see, she was hyperactive, and did all the things she hadn't been able to do before. Above all, her social calendar was very full because lots of people wanted to meet her and be reassured about the shaman's miracles.

On our part, we wanted to know when we could see this famous aunt and expressed our disappointment. So Tape Recorder said, 'That's just what I was coming to when you interrupted me. My aunt has given me detailed instructions for getting to the shaman's village. Apparently we can go directly to him without passing through my aunt if we can prove our case is urgent. You just need to get together half the money he's asking.' That is, 100,000 Malian francs. The money had to be put directly into the shaman's hands. Zani didn't understand why the fact that we had to pay half the money to the shaman directly would make us privileged customers if the waiting list was so long. My uncle asked Nostra.

'Nostra, are you really sure about this business?'

'If my aunt hadn't been cured, I wouldn't be mixed up in

it. No one's forcing you to go and see the shaman. If you're not sure, we won't go. Pardon me, Amadou, but my two eyes work very well. I've no interest in this affair, I just wanted to help Amadou. But if you don't want to, it's not a problem.'

'Keep your hair on, we just want to be sure we're not throwing 100,000 francs out of the window. There are some pretty tall stories in Bamako and some tall-storytellers...'

'OK, then, give me time to get my aunt to meet you. She'll probably be able to at the end of the week.'

Once we saw the soles of Tape Recorder's shoes, we all said what we thought. Zani was the first to say that he no longer believed a word of the story. My uncle followed suit. As for me, I was sure we couldn't trust Nostradamus. We changed the subject by playing together until dusk. When I got home, I told my parents about the episode with Tape Recorder. My mother changed her mind when she learned the shaman wanted money up front. My father laughed and the subject was dropped.

Chapter Nine
War and Music

A week after this episode, we were awoken one morning by explosions and tanks. My sisters climbed onto the wall of our house to look at the city in the distance. They saw people running in all directions to get to safety. We heard terrified children crying. Bamako was in turmoil. A state of emergency had been declared. Troops were ordered to be in uniform and armed. My father said all military barracks were on high alert. In the market, merchants closed their shops. There were tanks at every roundabout and bridge.

It was November 1968. Lieutenant Moussa Traoré and his henchmen were taking power by force. The civilian government of the socialist President Modibo Keïta was on its way out, toppled by a group of young army officers later to be called the CMLN (Military Committee for National Liberation). A lights-out curfew covered Bamako and the rest of Mali from ten at night until morning. My father had certain sympathies with this revolutionary group, but he did not approve of the coup. The violent takeover of power made him uneasy. What's more, he feared a civil war because he knew there were divisions among the coup leaders, and he didn't think the CMLN could change things in Mali anyway.

A few days after the coup, a handful of former government ministers and some business leaders were arrested and jailed. Uncertainty and fear were rife. Throughout this dark period, all cultural activities were suspended. Bands couldn't play in public. On occasions, in certain areas, musicians were even punished for playing at home.

1968 seemed endless. But the civil war my father feared didn't materialise, thank God, and the country slowly returned to normal. We celebrated the New Year joyfully.

In early 1970, Zani formed a band in which I sometimes played the guitar and sang. The group was called 'Harmonica Jazz' because the main instruments were harmonicas and guitars. It was nicknamed National Orchestra C. We performed at various events. I remember one particular evening organised by the theatre troupe of Mamadou Badian Kouyaté, brother of the well known Malian writer, Seydou Badian Kouyaté. We hadn't asked for police permission to play after midnight because we were relying on our host's contacts. But a few jealous malcontents informed the police and it wasn't long before they raided the place with whips and batons. The guests defended themselves by throwing stones. The musicians bolted and I was left, on stage, scared stiff, not knowing what to do. I heard the police shout, 'Get out! Everybody out!' But uncharacteristically, one of the policemen figured out I was blind and instead of hitting me, he took my hand and talked to me. He was very nice and even drove me home to Bagadadji. Some of my fans, when they saw me leaving with a policeman, got angry because they thought I was being arrested and started throwing stones at the car I was being bundled into.

As well as stones, I heard insults. They were magnificently foul mouthed. I couldn't help laughing when I heard one of them say, 'You bastards, you're robots, you beat us up just like that. Mali doesn't belong to you, you know. We think with our brains, you just think with your big fat comma-shaped arses.' I was expecting a really vitriolic response from the cops whose verbal brutality and vulgarity are notorious in Mali. But they laughed and said, 'Thanks, bloody morons. Bet your dirty arses, and your ancestors, aren't as small as your little "fingers" and not as straight as a ruler! That do you?'

I got home safe and sound that night and the next day we laughed about what had happened. I played so much guitar during that period that I couldn't honestly say exactly when I turned into the guitarist I had dreamed of being. Being on stage became my normal everyday existence. As the Bambara proverb goes, 'This is my friend, that's his friend, and that there is his friend's friend. That's how the houses of friendship fill up.' In effect, all the friends I made were friends from the music world. All my mates were musicians. When we got together, we just couldn't stop playing. The curfew had been lifted and we were free to devote ourselves to our passion.

One weekend evening, a few of us were hanging out in the street outside my house in Bagadadji. Gaoussou Kiyassou Traoré, known as Jeff, who had also helped me learn the guitar and who often played bits of James Brown, Mamadou Samaké, nicknamed Boya, Tapa Sangaré or MTC, The Bear, and myself, had got out our *tjoumbas*, our acoustic guitars, and our timbales, and begun jamming.

Passing youngsters stopped to listen to us, some of them tried out a few dance moves to attract the girls.

And that's how Bagadadji, our acoustic band, was born, performing in the street at weekends. Our audience, made up primarily of young people, grew and grew, and eventually space became a problem. In early 1970, we were asked to perform with a band being formed in the Niaréla neighbourhood. We agreed, and joined Bourou Wara, which means Lion in Bambara, known as Julien Clerc, who played bass, Seydou Bagayogo, known as Michel Polnareff, who sang, Siramakan Sacko, otherwise known as Antoine, who also sang, Kiyassou alias Jeff on accompanying guitar, Old Sangaré or Old Bah, nicknamed El Grande, who sang Cuban songs, and Abdoulaye Bléni (*Bléni* means Red) called Blaise and nicknamed Brian Jones, on the *tjoumba*. There was also another singer from Bagadadji, Mamoutou Bagayago, alias Mamoutou Bah. We rehearsed in the playground of the school in Niaréla. Youngsters came to watch and our audience of fans swelled. Our fame reached areas of Bamako we hadn't even been to. We performed at weddings and other festivities all over the capital.

The country was still ruled by the young army officers who had taken power in 1968. The Niaréla band came under the jurisdiction of two ministers responsible for young people, Fa Bilé Samaké and Mamou Niaré. Schools in Bamako opened and closed their doors without anyone ever asking themselves if I could be a pupil. There was still no institute for teaching blind people. People who knew me well noticed that I always played with more intensity when the school term started. It may well have been my way of getting rid of my frustration at not being able to enjoy the same education as other youngsters my age.

With the help of my uncle, Zani and Addès, I joined the state sponsored ensemble the National Orchestra B, where I was a sort of apprentice musician. It was supposed to be less good than the National Orchestra A. The youth director, Kélétiqui Diabaté, gave me a lot of support. I played alternately with the National Orchestra B and in small groups like the Niaréla band. It was as if I was practising in the small bands the theory that I was learning in the Orchestra B, with which I played more important venues.

I sang well, I played the guitar and the flute, my musical knowledge was increasing and my technical level was improving. I was better than the musicians in the small bands I played in, so I began spending more time with the Orchestra musicians. I wanted to improve. The ones I saw most were Modibo Kané, whom we called Modibo Tjoumba, Bob and Amadou Traoré, who both sang, Balla who played the saxophone and sang, Madou Dia Tounkara on the solo guitar, Issa Tounkara on the bass, Mama Sissoko, son of Djeli Baba Sissoko, West Africa's great storyteller, who played the accompanying guitar, and finally someone I could not fail to mention because of his profession: his name was Adama and he sold bread and mayonnaise so we called him Adama Mayonnaise. He played a Cuban instrument called a *guiro* which is a sort of animal horn played with a bit of metal. In the intervals we ate the mayonnaise bread that Adama very kindly brought us.

I was no longer ashamed to call myself a musician. I

knew I was surrounded by good instrumentalists and I was aware that I'd learned a lot about music. I was proud that all the great musicians in Bamako knew me. My disability hadn't prevented me from developing talents that sighted people admired. My hearing was so good I could distinguish a Gibson guitar, an acoustic guitar and a Fender Stratocaster. I had something else unique: I was one of the few musicians who could recognise the precise provenance of pieces of Malian music, the region they came from – Kayes, Bamako, Sikasso, Ségou, Mopti, Gao and Timbuktu. I had a soft spot for music from Sikasso. I was a fan of Mamadou Sangaré, alias Madou Guitar, who sang and played his instrument beautifully.

Chapter Ten
A New Beginning

I enjoyed my life in Bamako. Kadett had asked Zani where I lived and found it by herself. She came to see me whenever she could. My mother, sisters and brothers all knew her and thought a lot of her. When she was there, I felt good. We usually talked about what was going on in the city, very rarely about music.

But one day, we learned my father was being transferred to Koutiala, in the Sikasso region. I was undecided. I didn't know whether I should go with my family or stay in Bamako. I felt comfortable in our neighbourhood, everybody knew me. I had made friends and spent part of my free time with Kadett who came to visit me with her friends. I was involved in lots of things in Bamako, both with my friends and the bands I played in.

The leaving date drew nearer and I still hadn't made up my mind. My parents asked if I had made my decision, if I was going with them or staying to play music with Zani, Addès and Uncle Madou. I needed time to think. But Zani and my uncle told me my parents needed me and talked of all the opportunities I'd find in Sikasso. Kadett also said she'd come to Koutiala in the holidays and stay with one of her aunts. So I told my father I would follow them.

On the morning of 16 July, 1970, I set off for Koutiala on-board a huge pick-up truck to join my parents. Passengers and bags were piled up in the back, or rather the passengers were on top of the bags. It was far from comfortable, but the atmosphere was extraordinary. I played my guitar the whole journey. The passengers were happy to listen, requesting first one song then another. And I was more than happy to oblige.

In Koutiala, the Civic Service had given us a house in the CAR camp about thirty kilometres from the town. I had to find my bearings in this new environment. Disability makes you grow up quickly. I had perfected a way of finding my way around by imagining things with increasing precision. In no time, I managed to find the toilets, the kitchen or my room, by myself. This might seem derisory if you can see, but for blind people it is huge. Unlike our last move, when I wasn't totally blind, I was now more sensitive to smells, noises, touch. I was more sensitive to the night air, birdsong, or the hardness of the earth I was walking on. My life revolved around a world I sensed. In the house, I sometimes bumped into something my brothers and sisters hadn't put away and this irritated my father.

A few days after my arrival in Koutiala, I received a visit from my friend Soungalo 'The Bear' Sanaogho, who was from the town. He was a bit older than me but had a brother, Bréhima, of my age. Bréhima was very funny, he was continually saying silly things like 'The Good Lord will make an exception of me. He will spare me death by keeping me eternally young. I am the most handsome and elegant man on earth!' He made us laugh a lot. We nicknamed him 'Young'. I spent a lot of my spare time with him.

Because of the distance between the CAR camp and the town centre, The Bear and Young suggested I lodge with them. My parents agreed so I moved in. We played music almost every day. The Bear wasn't a professional musician, he wasn't interested in playing in a band, but he loved the harmonica. Slowly, the number of musicians wanting to play with us grew. We sat outside the front door to play, like in Bamako.

One day, a musician who was a tailor and was called Yayi Djané, came to join our group. He suggested I play in the Koutiala orchestra, Koulistar. I thought it was a good idea. So he introduced me to the orchestra leader, Seydou Koné, who was a schoolteacher as well. He played the *tjoumba* and sang songs in Mignanga, the language spoken by a tribe in the Koutiala region. Seydou, The Bear and I hit if off straight away. We would play in front of the house, and the word spread around town. People came to see us, encourage us and leave us a few coins. Others, I have to admit, insulted us and told us that Koutiala girls would never look at us. But The Bear replied, 'OK, Mr Alcohol, we've got your message, we'll bear it in mind!'

One afternoon, while The Bear, Young and myself were drinking Malian tea in the shade of a mango tree in the patio of our house, two men came to see us. They were both local dignitaries in Koutiala. They introduced themselves as Mamadou Doumbia and Zoumana Traoré, known as Zou, responsible for the city council's young people's affairs. They said they had heard about our concerts and hoped that I would become part of Koulistar. They managed the orchestra and said they wanted to make it both bigger and better. Monsieur Doumbia had a son of my age who was sound in body and mind, and he told me he often compared him to me. He thought I was much braver, and that my disability had made me strong. He said, 'My son sits on his backside all day, holds out his hand and says "Papa, give me money." He loves music but doesn't practise, he spends his life dreaming of a life that he cannot afford.'

He then explained that, because the orchestra was sponsored by the council, I would have to take various tests before I could join. I would get a small remuneration too. I also learned that the orchestra got together twice a week, on Fridays and Saturdays, to give paid concerts for people. The entrance-ticket money went into the kitty of the Young People's Office in Koutiala and was then shared out among the orchestra members. The Bear, who was older than me, replied to the proposal of Monsieurs Doumbia and Zoumana thus:

'We thank you for coming all this way to make Amadou this offer. I personally wanted him to be part of Koulistar. But you must realise that it's not easy for Amadou to get about. So we will also have to ask his father what he thinks.'

'As far as getting about is concerned, we will bring him home after every concert. As for his parents, we can go and see them right away.'

The Bear agreed to go to the CAR camp. We all went off to my father's house. Before he made his decision, he asked the two men a lot of questions, and also asked me what I thought. I was full of enthusiasm, so he said yes. The discussion went on for some time. They agreed to fetch me the following Friday.

The very next day, we began rehearsing some James Brown and Laba Sosseh songs, not forgetting some of my own compositions that my own small audience liked listening and dancing to. I was a bit nervous because I didn't know how the orchestra and the fans would react to my disability. I tried to remember all the advice people had given me. I prepared for the test.

On the fateful day, I tuned my acoustic guitar, and The Bear chose my best clothes from my bag. A car came to get me in the late afternoon to take me to Kokô, a neighbourhood behind the creek which ran through part of the town. Koulistar was going to play at the local town hall. When we arrived, the instruments were all on stage, the die was cast.

We downed some soft drinks and the ensemble filed past me to introduce themselves. I met Boubacar Ouattara, known at Ouatt, a guitarist, Boniface Dembélé, another guitarist, Mamadou Dembélé, called Jeo, who would later leave the band and I'd replace him on the solo guitar, Téningou Diarra, who played the *tjoumba*, Mamadou alias Mad 13, who played the timpani, Papa Gnangue, the main singer, Solodjan, which means Big Solo in Bambara, known as Josef, who did the backing with Massa, Old Sangaré who had come from Bamako to play the saxophone, Abdoulaye Bah, called Batch, a drummer, and orchestra leader Seydou Koné, a saxophonist who also played the bass guitar on occasions.

Monsieur Doumbia took my hand and led me on stage. The band's electric guitar awaited me. I knew I had at least two fans in the audience, The Bear and Young. I played a James Brown piece, 'Mother Popcorn'. The others joined in and I knew, instinctively, that I'd passed the test. I have to admit the Koutiala orchestra wasn't on the same level as the one in Bamako. When the concert ended, there was huge applause. The audience was hysterical and kept shouting 'Encore'. They didn't want us to leave. They would have liked us to play till dawn. Monsieurs Zou and Doumbia told me afterwards that they hoped to make an exception and give me a monthly salary of 400 Malian francs. They assured me that the other musicians had agreed. They gave me my first salary straight away.

We went home to tell my parents the good news, and they suggested I give half to the town's poor and use the rest to buy milk for a *daiguai*, a dish of boiled semolina. We shared it with the whole neighbourhood. It was a way of thanking God and our ancestors for having honoured us, and made my music successful. And to pray that my name would cross mountains and oceans, and that the whole of Mali would be proud to call me their native son.

And that was my Koutiala orchestra debut. We played in the town hall every weekend. I actually began to get a bit of reputation in the area. When I walked in the street with one of The Bear's brothers, people would give us presents and ask me to sign autographs. I heard tell that certain girls wanted to get in contact with me. It was all very pleasant. At the end of our first year in Koutiala, Kadett came to visit her aunt. She managed to spend a few days with me at The Bear and Young's house. She took the trouble to go and say hello to my parents who had no idea what we were getting up to. They imagined she was a friend of one of my sisters.

Neither of us was eighteen yet. According to Malian customs, my parents could have reproached me for my behaviour, and they would have been perfectly within their rights. That's why we preferred to hide it from them and keep up the 'friend of my sister' pretence.

In time, I became an integral part of the Koutiala orchestra. I knew all the musicians and they never minded helping me. I got on especially well with Ouatt. We spent a lot of time together. Later I met other members of the Youth Department, like Sékou Traoré, N'Fa Kamissogo and Gnara Sidibé who worked at Koutiala council. Thanks to him, the council agreed to give me a bit more money. Gnara had a battery-charged record player. He, Baba Bagayogo, known as B Squared, Alassane Touré alias Mister Minister, Abdou 'Gean' N'Diaye and myself, listened to all the new music their friends in the US sent them.

The orchestra flourished. Monsieur Doumbia put in for a council grant for money to buy new instruments. We rehearsed regularly and trained particularly hard for the Sikasso Regional Youth Week. Ouatt had told me about the Sikasso orchestra which, according to him, was a real professional orchestra. He also said that during Youth Week, a prize would be given to the best musician in each instrumental category and that the prize-winners would be invited to join the official Sikasso ensemble, one of the ones that would be performing before the President of Mali and all his ministers at the Bamako Biennale.

My heart skipped a beat. I wanted it to happen to me one day. The local papers already had lots of articles about us,

Koulistar. They were mostly complimentary except when there was trouble with girls. Ouatt got snared by a newspaper that published photos of him with different girls. His official girlfriend found out and took it pretty badly. His 'sweetheart' decided to punch him in the face. Ouatt went too far, but I wasn't an angel either. My disability allowed me to do more things because I was forgiven more easily. And also I looked innocent because I was blind.

The stories of scandal didn't bother Monsieurs Doumbia and Zou, who considered that bad publicity was publicity all the same. While these stories about chicks were going around, we were practising hard for the Sikasso festival. I perfected my pieces and rehearsed with Ouatt. I practised voice exercises at every opportunity. We had no reason to lament a shortage of money because our fans provided it every weekend by throwing coins onto the stage. We collected them up and divided them equally among us. Apart from those who had too many children, too many women, or problems with the bailiffs, no one in the orchestra had money problems.

I had got completely used to being blind by now. I relied on what I understood best, my memory and my imagination. The pleasure of music was what made my world go round. People always remarked when I had composed a new song, and I received special encouragement. But I was apprehensive about the Sikasso concert. I hoped our orchestra would be the best in the region. Two dancers, a girl and a boy, were to enhance our show.

Chapter Eleven
Applause

The day finally arrived. I got in an air-conditioned car that took three hours to get to the concert. Ouatt didn't stop complaining about the car's speed, comparing it to a chameleon. In the hotel where Ouatt and I shared a room, Monsieur Doumbia gave us a sermon in which he set out all the hopes he put in us. Several groups went on stage before us. Some were quite good but made mistakes, others were plain bad. When it was our turn, the audience, who didn't know us, were astonished and delighted to see a blind guitarist as part of the group. Sympathy for disabled people, in Mali and many other African countries I know, is very good.

When the drummer tapped his sticks together, we all waved and started playing to thunderous applause. By the third song, the audience was making the ground shake with all their jumping. When our set was over, the crowd wanted us to do two of the songs again. Apparently the governor of the region got out of his seat for the first time to applaud us. The reaction was excellent. Journalists came to interview us.

Later that night, people described the furore our performance had caused. The audience had tears in their eyes while we were playing. We realised we had been one of the best groups, and hoped we'd be leaving with a prize.

The governor sent a messenger over to me with an invitation to dine at his residence the following day. When I asked why, he said that the governor had a proposition for me. My friends told me to be very careful because politicians always try to get some personal advantage out of everything; that he probably wanted to appear in the newspaper beside a blind youngster. The most virulent comments came from Monsieur Doumbia, and I reminded him that he was a politician too. He challenged me to name a better-managed band than Koulistar. Later he told me that certain people were saying that my success was down to my disability. 'But,' he said, 'don't listen to them, the guitar is your thing and you play it really well. You practise hard and take music very seriously. People say whatever comes into their heads. Just believe in yourself, and you'll go far. Tomorrow, listen to what the governor proposes.'

I was a bit worried by what he'd said. It was the second time people had linked my success to my disability. This gossip was nasty and I was hurt by what was said. People's expressions didn't bother me because I couldn't see them, but I knew whether people felt sympathy or antipathy towards me by the tone of their voice. One day Zani had alluded to quarrels that break out among musicians because of jealousy. He added that the ones who got on best were those who didn't give a toss and let it all blow over them. I really couldn't tell if anyone in the group was hostile to me. I preferred not to think about it.

The next day, at 11.45am, I heard a car stop in front of the hotel. Ouatt whispered in my ear, 'Wow, Amadou, that's classy. It's a jet-black Peugeot 404, air-conditioned for sure.

You can bet people who take their arses around in contraptions like that will be spared the Day of Reckoning. Music's going to take you up to heaven anyway.'

I got into the back of the car and from that moment was treated like a prince. The car was well and truly air-conditioned: so much so that I was freezing. On the way, the chauffeur told me a bit about his boss, that he was very interested in the less fortunate because he was from a poor background himself. The chauffeur had got a raise, for instance, without even having to ask for it. Then he told me to forget what he had just told me because he wasn't supposed to reveal information about the governor.

The governor was very charming to me. He received me in his beautiful house, with his wife and children. He introduced himself first, and told me to call him Sory Ibrahima Sylla. We all ate together, then the children went upstairs to do their homework and Monsieur Sylla explained the reason for his invitation.

'I wanted to invite you to my home, with my family, because I'm impressed by your determination to want to make something of your life despite your disability. Here, we don't know any blind or paralysed people who have tried to get ahead, to have a trade. They prefer to sit at roundabouts and ask for charity. I was very moved by your performance on stage. It was a way of telling other disabled people "Look, you see, it is possible. You don't have to accept what happens to you. You can make something of your life."'

He then told me about a government project to create a school for young blind people. The French and Germans were ready to provide material for teaching Braille. They planned to have an orchestra in the school. That's why the governor was interested in me. He thought he could help me get into the school, if I wanted to. However, I would have to go back to Bamako because here, in Sikasso, there was nothing for people like me. I told the governor:

'Thank you for your concern. I must admit that people told me lots of things about you. But I don't make judgements because I can't see faces. God took my eyes but he has given me the gift of other senses. I sense that you want what is best for me and I thank you for it.'

And I began to tell him my story, how I became blind, how they'd tried to operate on me, how they'd discovered my trachoma, and how I'd finally been left in the dark.

After I finished, the governor talked about giving me a letter for his friend the governor of Bamako. I said I'd tell my parents about his proposition but that I was sure they'd agree to let me go to Bamako alone. I cited my musician friends with whom I'd almost stayed behind in the capital. I finally asked if he thought our orchestra would win the prize this year. He advised me to be patient. 'You know the old proverb that says "He who is faster than the music dances badly", so wait for the results at the end of the week.' When he said goodbye, he slipped a thousand-franc note into my hand and wished me good luck.

I was a little disappointed by the visit, because the governor had been rather cold when he talked about our exploits on stage the previous evening. His attitude naturally contrasted with Monsieur Doumbia's enthusiasm. I was afraid we wouldn't get a prize, that we hadn't managed to show we were the best. When I arrived back, Ouatt was eager to hear about my visit to the governor's house. He was waiting downstairs to take me to the rest of the group. They let rip with the jokes.

'So, did he ask you to write a song for him?'

'Have you been corrupted, Amadou? Did you get brainwashed?'

'No, he told me about a school for young blind people being created in Bamako that he might be able to help me get in to. I could learn to write and read music in Braille.'

'That's brilliant, Amadou.'

'No, Ouatt, it isn't. Amadou has only just joined our group and the governor suggests he leave us to follow some fantasy.'

'But, Monsieur Doumbia, you know that before he lost his sight Amadou used to go to school… If the governor can help him increase his knowledge of music, that's a good thing.'

Everyone agreed except Monsieur Doumbia, who referred to the success of groups like the Rolling Stones who, according to him, would never have split up under any circumstances. Then they asked me about the prize, what were our chances of winning. I had to disappoint them because the governor hadn't wanted to broach the subject. I understood our manager's anxiety about my leaving the group for the Blind Institute. But back in our bedroom Ouatt insisted I mustn't lead my life according to what Monsieur Doumbia said, because obviously his main interest was his group. He reminded me that Doumbia had advised me not to go and see the governor, and now he was trying to influence me not to get an education. Ouatt said that Doumbia wasn't interested in our future and encouraged me to apply for the blind school.

Relations with our manager remained a bit strained until the prize-giving. That day, Monsieur Doumbia was so nervous that Ouatt whispered to me that he wasn't sure he'd survive if the news was bad. After a short speech, the governor was supposed to hand envelopes and trophies to the winners. Ouatt gave me a running commentary on what was happening on stage. I was less stressed than the others since I couldn't see what everyone was doing. The judging criteria were varied: the group's performance, their empathy with the audience, choreography, song lyrics... They began by reading out the names of the groups who hadn't won prizes. We weren't on that list.

In fact, we did win first prize. Monsieur Doumbia mounted the podium to receive it from the governor. And then I went up, because I had won the prize for the best guitarist in Sikasso! I was handed a microphone to say a few words. I didn't know what to say but all of a sudden someone put a guitar round my neck. So I played. It wasn't easy because with all the shouting from the audience, I couldn't hear myself play. Then I thanked everyone and left the stage. The governor came up and congratulated me personally. He embraced me. I told him how grateful I was but he brushed it aside and said I owed it all to my hard work.

That day was one of the most wonderful days of my life. I was eighteen and recognised as a talented musician. As winners, the group had to bring the evening to a close. We played the six songs that had made us laureates. The party went on long into the night. Journalists wanted to interview me and take photos. The next day, we heard the whole town of Koutiala was waiting for us with more celebrations. A reception had been planned with all the town's dignitaries. While we were waiting to leave, the governor phoned me. He proposed taking me to Koutiala in his car so he could meet my parents and get their permission. He said I could bring a friend from the group with me. But obviously I had to ask Monsieur Doumbia first. The governor said he would take care of it. We heard our manager say very politely, 'Yes, of course, that's fine, Governor, no problem at all, Governor, as you wish, Governor.' Ouatt thought it was all a great joke, saying he wanted to ride with me in the car where people never died.

When Monsieur Doumbia came back into the room, he didn't look at all happy. He suspected the governor wanted to bask in our group's glory in our town. He held forth endlessly on the subject. Ouatt tried to calm him down and convince him the governor's aims weren't so cynical, but he wouldn't listen to him. He insisted.

'I know that, for someone like you, shaking the hand of the governor of this region is a dazzling experience. But all these great titles they deck themselves out in come and go. So, be careful. It's easy to come down to earth, like you and me…'

'Like me, perhaps, but not like you. There's an enormous difference between us. You're the head of the council's youth programme and director of the youth club. I'm just a simple musician in the Koutiala orchestra.'

Monsieur Doumbia's mistrust of Governor Sylla had created a bad atmosphere in the group. Ouatt said Doumbia was jealous. It didn't stop me travelling in one of the governor's cars with Ouatt. We chatted with the chauffeur, Ibrahim Sangaré. He recognised Monsieur Doumbia's talents as manager and organiser, and I agreed. But Ouatt thought I was exaggerating. 'What are you talking about, Amadou? He should thank us for our self-sacrifice and devotion. The instruments don't play themselves. I know orchestras made up of serious, able musicians, but as soon as they get a bit of fame, they start drinking and whoring. But us, we're very serious.' The chauffeur was astonished that we could talk about it so calmly.

'How do you manage to keep your cool?'

'D'you really think we're cool?'

'Seems like it.'

'Have you ever heard that appearances are deceptive.'

Chatting pleasantly, we devoured the kilometres that separated us from Koutiala. At one stage, we caught up with the musicians' bus that had left an hour before us. But the convoy of the governor's cars never overtook the bus for reasons of diplomacy. Monsieur Doumbia was not to be crossed.

When we finally arrived, after following the bus for ages, Koutiala was jubilant. We could hear shouting, drumming, moped horns, car horns, bicycle bells. Out of his mind with joy, Ouatt said he'd never seen so many people in the streets, and what a pity it was that I couldn't see the crowd that had come to celebrate our exploits. I reassured him that while my eyes couldn't see it, my heart could; that I could feel the crowd pulsating around us. It was very beautiful and moving for me to sense all that. The crush of people was such that Ouatt was worried we wouldn't be able to get out of the car. He waited for some soldiers to control the crowd. The car finally managed to make its way towards the camp where there was another crowd of villagers.

In front of our house, my brothers and sisters rushed forward to congratulate me and get my bags out of the trunk. I didn't have time to count the number of people who kissed me. All this effusiveness lasted for some time. Malian tradition demands that before greeting the traveller you have to bring him fresh water. Normally, it's one of the daughters of the house who goes to the well for water that she keeps in an earthenware jar. These jars are a very important component of everyday African life. They are kept in the shade and contain everything the family is going to eat.

There's no point asking the traveller if he is thirsty. We work on the principle that he is bound to need refreshment. He has the right to refuse if it so happens that he isn't thirsty, but he must all the same pretend to drink and give the daughter of the house back her jar. The task falls to a young girl because it's a way of encouraging marriages. If she isn't already spoken for, she could marry the traveller and widen the horizons of her family.

My sisters were in charge of giving us water. And, after the usual long polite exchanges, a conversation took place between my father and Governor Sylla. The latter dominated it for a long time, explaining in detail what he had planned for me. He talked about an institute for young blind people being set up by a certain Monsieur Konaté, who himself was blind, and funded by the government. He insisted that it was crucial for a musician to be able to read and write music in Braille. He defined Braille for my parents, 'A conventional alphabet written with protruding points that can equally be applied to numbers, letters and music.' He assured my parents that there was absolutely no personal gain in it for him, and that his only wish was to help me. His father had gone blind at the end of his life.

In turn, my father thanked the governor. He told him that the last time there was talk of my staying in Bamako, things had been different because I was still a minor. Now I was eighteen and he was sure that it was better for me to be in the capital. And that, whatever I decided, I would have his blessing. My parents invited the governor and his family to share our meal. My brothers went off to catch two chickens in our yard. At a certain moment, Ouatt and I found ourselves together in my room. He said, 'What you lost with your eyes, the Good Lord has given you back in luck. You have the luck of a hyena. She is reputed to be the luckiest of all animals. I'll come to Bamako with you and accompany you on the great path to the stars you've already embarked on. We'll sign huge contracts and romance superb chicks, but not long enough for the newspapers to accuse us of polygamy!'

There was a great atmosphere during the meal. Everybody was happy. When the governor and his family had taken their leave, my father shared his astonishment with me.

'Until now, I was *a priori* prejudiced against musicians. I thought they never had a penny, they drank a lot and always had dubious liaisons with girls. They couldn't take responsibility for a family. I often talked about it with your Uncle Madou. But now, a governor has come to my house, and he has given me an envelope that bears witness to my son's talent. I am very surprised and very proud. Amadou, you have convinced me, we believe in you, we support you. We are all very moved by your success.'

At this point I was assailed by my brothers and sisters who wanted to know all about the minor miracles we'd worked during the competition week. They said my incipient fame reflected on them.

On the other hand, I was surprised to note that, apart from Ouatt, none of the orchestra came to see me. I sensed a certain tension that I could do nothing about. I also wondered why Monsieur Doumbia hadn't come. I tried to rationalise it by telling myself that one can't save something that is already doomed to failure. That's when Ouatt came and gave me an account of what was going on behind my back. Monsieur Doumbia was busy criticising me, saying I was allowing a politician to manipulate me. I was shocked and wanted to go and see Monsieur Doumbia but Ouatt talked me out of it by reminding me that, 'If a man wants to kill his dog, he accuses him of having rabies.' And, common sense prevailing, he added that if this man was capable of dropping us for such a feeble motive, he wasn't very solid and his orchestra wouldn't go very far. He thought that the most important thing wasn't the sympathy of individuals but the sympathy of the public. That's what makes successful artists.

As for the musicians, Ouatt confessed they were jealous of my prize for best guitarist and that no matter how much they congratulated me and pretended they were my friends, in actual fact they hated me; for the simple reason that I was the best musician. In this group, there was too much jealousy. I suffered doubly because it wasn't my fault. Ouatt reminded me that you can't live in peace with a neighbour who doesn't want to live in peace with you.

Chapter Twelve
Glory and Jealousy

A few days later, Monsieur Doumbia came to see me. The conversation was frosty. We didn't mention what had happened. He said that the orchestra had been invited to perform in a smart restaurant by a general and two ministers. He seemed delighted and very proud. I asked him if the ministers weren't those same politicians for whom he had such disdain. I had a burning desire to refuse the offer but I preferred to say I'd let him know tomorrow. He was irritated by my hesitation and tried to convince me not to spoil the group's chances by not coming.

It's not in my nature to hold grudges. I don't know if it's to do with my disability, which has taught me patience, but I gave Monsieur Doumbia another chance and accepted his proposition. Ouatt came to see me. The manager had called on him too. I laughed as he said:

'It reminds me of the monkeys and crocodiles story. OK, there was this group of monkeys, led as usual in the monkey kingdom by the strongest monkey. In the rutting season, the leader wanted to be alone with all the females, so he thought up a ruse. On the river bank, he suggested to the others that he go on ahead, on the pretext of negotiating with the females. He also warned them of the crocodiles lurking in the river and advised that while some monkeys drank, the others watched the flow of the river. They took his advice, and the crocodiles didn't get a bite to eat. They were furious because they were hungry. They mocked the monkeys who were sitting calmly in the trees waiting for their leader and their ladies: "The Good Lord gave you a raw deal. He put no hair on your bums so ants bite you when you sit on branches!" The monkeys didn't know what to say until their leader came back with the ladies, and retorted: "The Good Lord has nothing against monkeys; hairy or not, at least we can sit on our bums, unlike you lot. God stuck huge tails on your backs and immense evil-smelling holes where you relieve yourselves!" The other animals watching this exchange between monkeys and crocodiles roared with laughter. The moral of this story is that crocs would like to sit on their bums like monkeys but their tails won't let them. Monsieur Doumbia is a crocodile who'd like to be the politicians he criticises.'

We had a long discussion about politicians. We agreed they weren't all corrupt and rotten, that some sincerely wanted to improve the state of the country they were responsible for.

The concert for the ministers was scheduled for the following weekend. Our fans got wind of the gig and stationed themselves at the entrance to the restaurant. The soldiers tried to appeal for calm. But it was hard to have lunch in peace because of the racket that was going on outside the door. During lunch, I was the centre of attention. I was seated between the two ministers, who asked me to tell my story.

They too had decided to help me. And thanks to them, the orchestra went to record in the studios of the Malian national radio. Our songs were soon playing on the radio every day. Ouatt joked that we now belonged to Malian history. The two ministers, General Amadou Baba Diarra and Karim Dembéle, were important for me. My relationship with Amadou, my namesake, became a deep and lasting friendship. He and his lovely wife Lala Coulibaly helped me a lot. They gave me money and lots of encouragement.

At the end of that year, the orchestra made up of all the musicians who had won prizes in Sikasso, came together again. I heard it said somewhere that when God decides something is going to happen, it happens whether human beings want it or not. And that what is going to fail, will fail no matter what efforts are made here on earth. During the biennale in Bamako, I had a premonition that a big career awaited me. When I rejoined the orchestra in Sikasso, everyone reinforced this idea. Governor Sylla came to see me and confirmed the move to Bamako. He said the time was right for me to come and live in the capital. I told him I was seriously interested in doing so.

Back in Koutiala, I announced my wish to continue my career in Bamako. My parents and I set the date for me to move back in 1973. My mother admitted she felt ambivalent about it. One the one hand she was happy I was going to be independent, that I would not have to depend on charity. On the other, she was sad at having to say goodbye, at seeing me leave. The evening before my departure, we had a big party and danced. I tried to persuade Ouatt to come to Bamako with me. He wasn't very keen because he was nervous about the political situation in the capital, which he compared to a powder keg because it was so unstable. He was sure that the soldiers who had taken power by force would not be able to keep it. What you get by violence you have to retain by violence. People were showing signs of impatience. The government had not kept its positive image for very long.

When the big day came, the whole town was at the station to say goodbye. The weather still wasn't too hot. It was the first time I'd ever travelled without my family. It was the big voyage of emancipation, I was going to fly with my own wings. My family was sad, but knew it was best for me, that this would broaden my horizon. I got into the railway carriage and slept for the whole journey. I was exhausted. A taxi dropped me at Uncle Madou's house. I was so happy to be with him again! We exchanged our latest news. They had followed my exploits in Sikasso on the radio. Then he told me about his group, Les Ambassadeurs du Motel de Bamako; the members were all public servants. I recounted my meeting with the governor. He said, 'And the poor will be rich, the last will be the first, and the lowly will be great.'

After I'd washed, I went back and found my uncle preparing the oven for tea. He mysteriously asked me not to get in touch with Zani. I never understood why. He gave me some bad news: Kadett had got married and gone to live in Gabon with her husband. He then confessed he wasn't as close as he used to be to his musician friends, their success had gone to their heads. I was well placed to understand what Madou meant: jealousy, vanity… I gave him a rundown of what had happened with Monsieur Doumbia and Governor Sylla.

He had decided that the best thing would be for me to start playing with the Motel Ambassadors. He took me to see one of his acquaintances, Yamadou Diallo, who seemed to know the music scene pretty well. He spent a long time congratulating me on my courage. He said joining the Ambassadors was a good choice because it was the best group in Bamako after the Rail Band, especially since some of its members could write music. He and I then went to see the manager of the Motel Ambassadors, Monsieur Makalou. He accepted me straight away because he had heard of me. All the same, he wanted to try me out with the other musicians to be absolutely sure of my level. Monsieur Makalou wanted to take me home but I preferred to take a taxi, so he wouldn't figure out I was Embassy's nephew. I didn't want any problems, I didn't want anything to diminish my chances of joining this group.

The day of the audition, my uncle didn't come with me. Kanté Manfila was there, he said he'd help convince them and try to get them to let me sing the Cuban songs. They asked for 'El Manisero' and a French song I didn't know very well, 'Kati, Kati'. I was impressed by how good the group was straight away. Their sound was excellent and they never lost the rhythm, you could've taken them for metronomes. I didn't sing too badly. At the end, Monsieur Makalou called me over and said, 'Amadou, you're really intelligent, but you've a lot to learn about the repertoire – tango, morena, bossa nova, merengue jazz, and the rest – and about playing in a band. So, at first, I suggest you work for free. When you've improved, we'll start paying you.'

I accepted the post of apprentice musician and Kanté

100

helped me improve my guitar technique. The group was made up of Issa Niaré on bass guitar, Idrissa Soumaoro on keyboard, Salif Keïta who sang the Mandingo repertory, Moussa Doumbia, alias James, who sang James Brown and Otis Redding songs and some rock too, and Ousmane Dia who sang in French and in Wolof. The head honcho was Issiaka Dama, drummer, flautist and singer.

I made very fast progress and it wasn't long before I was on the payroll. I marvelled at how far I'd come, I compared little Amadou from Koutiala to the person I was now. My musical dexterity had clearly improved. I now had a friend, Cheick Tidiane Seck, who was also taking classes with Kanté. We helped each other. We bought books about music from the street booksellers where you found all sorts of stuff, including books stolen from libraries. The police often made lightning raids to nab the thieves. But we had no choice because the books in proper shops were out of our price range. At first I wasn't too keen on moving in this slightly dodgy world, and not too proud of buying books obtained in a crooked way.

My friend read me these illicitly obtained works and Kanté patiently taught us the guitar and revelled in having us as pupils. Being hired by the group brought me the grand salary of twenty-five thousand Malian francs, not including tips. I was so happy I cried. My uncle was beside himself with joy and pride. He marked the event by inviting the whole group to his house. We spent a memorable moment of real camaraderie.

My first trip outside Malian borders was with the Motel Ambassadors; it was July of 1974. We were invited to tour France and we stayed two months. We played in Saint-Denis, Pantin, then Paris on the university campus and in the XIXth arrondissement in a club called Galaxie. I have fond memories of our hotel in the rue Doudeauville.

Back in Mali, at Uncle Madou's house, I was told that a certain Kindjan Diallo wanted to meet me. I knew his name because he had been a footballer and captain of the Eagles national team. He was now in charge of the sports stadium in Bamako. I went to Kindjan's office. He immediately took me off to see Monsieur Konaté, the man Governor Sylla had mentioned. He told me that during a recent womens' conference, the government had confirmed to him its support for the creation of an Institut de Jeunes Aveugles (IJA), an institute for young blind people.

Although Monsieur Konaté was himself blind, I had the impression that he paid great attention to the terms he used. He explained in detail what the IJA would be and told me how appropriate it was that I should be part of it. He described the advantages of the institute for me, the fact that I'd be able to learn Braille. Before listening to what I had to say, he stressed that there were still some places available, but that wouldn't be the case for long.

I replied, 'Thank you very much for your concern. But I have just joined a professional band, the Motel Ambassadors. I'm now getting a salary. I've spent a lot of time and effort getting to this stage. Changing now might be risky. Besides, I don't know how I'd feel surrounded by blind people like me. Up till now, I've always been with people who could see. On the other hand, I really want to learn Braille. At the moment, I'm learning music theory with a friend. He reads me books. Actually, I really need time to think about it.'

After we left Monsieur Konaté, I discussed it further with Monsieur Kindjan. At my uncle's house, he pronounced himself in favour of the Ambassadors. He thought it a pity to abandon everything I'd achieved, and declared, 'Every new path is difficult to walk.' He didn't want me to take the risk. Kanté, with whom I talked the following day, was all for me going to the IJA, arguing that, of the two, it was the most reliable and most enriching path. He saw that I could easily have a band of my own at the institute, but that being with the Ambassadors it would take much longer.

A long tour through Africa was planned for the Ambassadors. I was delighted by the idea of travelling, especially when it meant going to Guinea where I might shake the hand of my hero, President Sékou Touré, a respected revolutionary. We were at the height of the Cold War and Sékou had said no to the West. He had chosen Moscow and Socialism. His main slogan was, 'We prefer poverty with dignity to opulence with repression.' Some people said he was totally under Moscow's thumb. In any case, I liked his anti-colonialist stance and his interest in sport, music and politics. In his country there was active interest in all these three fields. Two Guinean groups, the Bembeya Jazz National and the Camayenne Sofa had a very good reputation all over Africa.

We landed in Conakry at about 11 o'clock in the morning. A car came to meet us at the airport and took us to the hotel.

To our great surprise, we learned that Badema National,

a national group, was also in Guinea. When President Sékou Touré came to Mali to calm the emotions of the presidents of Mali and Burkina Faso, (Moussa Traoré and Thomas Sankara who unfortunately had now been at war with each other for some days), the Motel Ambassadors had played for him in the sports stadium. He had really liked their music. So now we were in Guinea, and it wasn't long before we met the president. We were all intimidated by Sékou Touré's forceful personality. He greeted us all and praised our music. He spoke very well: very slowly and very distinctly. He turned to me in particular and repeated what I had already heard a thousand times: that people who didn't have my disability weren't as motivated as I was. He told us that he had invited us before when the Guinean army had beaten the Portuguese mercenaries. Portugal had in fact tried to overthrow the president who criticised their neo-colonialist attitude: he preferred fair and equitable relationships of cooperation. Before we left, he presented us with books he had written and gave us a real political speech.

I was lead guitarist for the whole of our Guinea tour. I'd been given that honorary role. When we got back to the capital, the president asked to see us again before we flew on to Ivory Coast. There, everything was much more comfortable but the welcome wasn't as warm. We continued on to Lagos, Nigeria, where we spent two days at a festival.

Back in Mali, I could no longer put off my answer to the blind institute. I went to visit it. Monsieur Konaté showed me round the premises. My uncle whispered that it all looked very nice and he was sure it would be a way forward for me. In the classrooms, Monsieur Konaté introduced me to the pupils as the famous musician from the Motel Ambassadors. At the end of the visit, I told the director I'd be delighted to enrol as a pupil at the IJA.

Chapter Thirteen
Mariam: Love at First Sight

When I enrolled in the school, it didn't have a proper orchestra, just what they called 'an artistic troupe'. It was all girls. Mariam Doumbia sang and other girls accompanied her, clapping or beating tam-tams. In those days, it hadn't occurred to Mariam that she could sing for a living. True, she wanted to be financially independent despite being blind, but she was more interested in dying cloth. In fact, a French woman called Anne Journaux had come to Mali to teach disabled girls how to dye, alongside Malian women like Kounandi Diakité and Mama.

There was lots of cultural activity at the institute. So, many important people were interested and supported it. Former President Traoré and his wife came regularly to see that the IJA was working smoothly. After listening to the 'troupe' for the first time, I suggested to Monsieur Konaté that I arrange some of Mariam's compositions. My real motivation was Mariam herself. Her beautiful voice, that is. I suggested we collaborate. She agreed and we began arranging some of her songs. I loved all of them. The lyrics touched me because they reflected her sadness and the hypocrisy with which society often treats disabled people. Because of a childhood illness, measles, which she caught when she was five, she had gradually lost her sight until she was now completely blind. She valued the opportunity she now had to learn Braille and stimulate her intellect. The founders of the institute in person had sought her out, through a neighbour Renée Diarra, and suggested she enrol. I asked her about her life, but I didn't want to intrude too much in case she thought I was interested in her. I got the impression she had suffered more than I had.

I realised how lucky I was that my parents had been so supportive from the very beginning. They didn't think twice about leaving Douansan for my sake, and had helped me all through the operation. My friends had been a big help too. I'd been welcomed everywhere I went. I couldn't fault anybody.

Of all Mariam's songs, the one that touched me most was 'Teree la sebin' (Certificate of Misfortune):

Aw ma né djo lé yé	You who see me before you
Ou yé sebin do né koukolo laaa	Have put in my head
Teree la sebin	A certificate of misfortune
Wolo ba sa ya ma folon né la	I'm not my mother's first orphan
Ga Ou yé sebin do né koukolo laaa	But you have unjustly put in my head
Teree la sebin	A certificate of misfortune
Sabou yé bana djougou yé	I blame nothing but my malady
Bana djougou dé yé né yan w minanaaa	The malady that made me blind

Mariam and I picked out the song on my guitar. With my melody, the lyrics sounded really good. So good in fact, that when Mariam sang it, my heart missed a beat. And we danced; a pleasure I'd never felt with the Motel Ambassadors.

At first I divided my time between the institute and the Ambassadors. But as my work with Mariam intensified, I had less time for them. Mariam and I decided to record

107

some of our songs at the studios of Radio Mali. The whole of Mali had been listening to them on the radio but there were no cassettes available. Someone remarked one day what an ideal couple Mariam and I would make. I hadn't thought of it before. The recording was the first time we'd been alone. I admit that my respect for her had grown as we worked together. I thought she was very nice and had a big heart. She always had time for the other young girls at the institute, helping them with intimate girls' things and other stuff.

Our cassettes came out, but distribution was limited to the local market. However, people talked about them a lot and Mariam's popularity grew in the areas Radio Mali was broadcast. I was getting more and more involved with the institute. They gave me a fold-up aluminium stick to help me get about. I learned to be more adroit and more agile.

One day, Monsieur Makalou came to see me at the institute to talk about my role in the Ambassadors. I had to decide if I was going to carry on with them. We mentioned the difficulties that had arisen with other members of the group who were jealous and teased me endlessly with things like, 'So, Amadou, you're rich from your cassettes now, you don't need what the Ambassadors pay you.' Monsieur Makalou told me to take no notice, it was par for the course with musicians. We decided I'd only play with the Ambassadors occasionally, so that I could concentrate more on the institute. I went in person to tell the other musicians and took the opportunity of thanking them all for having been so patient with a blind person.

At the institute, as well as making music with Mariam, Monsieur Konaté also asked me to write songs for the theatre group, to accompany the actors. I loved this role of training the students. I composed a lot of songs for Mariam and some for the other girls. When we rehearsed, the people who could see found us very beautiful.

We were invited to give our first concert in a hall dedicated to old soldiers. My father came from Koutiala to see me. There were loads of people. The hall was full and some people got their money back because all the seats were taken. In an orchestra, the idea isn't so much to play a symphony that's easy on the ear, but to create a bond between musicians, that each one brings a part of their genius. The great thing about music is the sharing. Mariam and I had that bond from the very first day we worked together. Because we couldn't see, our mutual admiration was founded on what we understood of each other, and especially on what we imagined.

One day, Monsieur Konaté asked us both to his office. He told us that the institute was flourishing and how happy he was with what we were contributing to this development. He also said we would be moving premises.

I'd left the Motel Ambassadors in 1979, although I continued meeting up with friends who still played in the band. One of them, Idrissa Soumaoro, a pianist, had even begun teaching at the institute. We played music together and ended up forming the band Eclipse. It was made up of Issa Niaré of the Ambassadors on bass, Idrissa on keyboard, Bah Tapo on drums, singer N'Golo Konaré, Mamadou

Keïta and Zoumana Cissé on the bongos. Some of the girls, Fatou Faye, Djoba Diarra and Jouma Keïta, did the backing.

The special thing about our group was that it mixed sighted and non-sighted people. We began getting noticed and Monsieur Konaté asked us to use the band to do some publicity for the institute. We even composed songs about how great the IJA was! And we recorded them at the radio studios. When they came onto the market, we received an avalanche of concert offers. We weren't in a position to accept all of them.

That year, 1980, Mariam lost her father, and we decided to slow down with the concerts. It rained so much in August that all the open air concerts had to be cancelled anyway. My career was taking its course. I heard The Ambassadors had split up. But Eclipse was going from strength to strength. Idrissa, who was a fine connoisseur of music, brought his knowledge and compositions to the group. All the songs were sung by Mariam who had acquired a whole range of vocal techniques at the institute. As for me, I was the solo guitarist I'd always dreamed of becoming. I didn't sing any more, that was Mariam's role.

She and I became so fond of each other that we needed to be with each other every day. When she wasn't there, I missed her. And the feeling was mutual. A seed of love was germinating. But we didn't talk about it openly yet. I thought about her all the time. What I felt for her was different from what I'd felt for girls before.

I realised I had to thank God for everything that had happened to me. I didn't have to rely on anyone financially, and my work was my passion. Life was very sweet. I played the guitar and drank Malian tea. When we weren't at the institute, Idrissa came to my house to work. One day, I finally told him about Mariam. He laughed and said it was not a secret, even the birds in the institute's trees knew how we felt. He said he was sure Mariam shared my feelings and advised me to open my heart. I told him of my fears. He promised to think about it. I didn't want to spoil everything because it could affect the group as well. I was glad I'd unburdened myself to Idrissa because my love for Mariam was like a spectre haunting me.

The director asked Eclipse members to intensify our campaign of spreading the word about the institute. He wanted us to take a travelling show round Mali. The money raised would go into the institute coffers. It would also silence certain students who thought the band members received special favours. I wasn't happy with that at all.

We went to the Kayes region, then on to Sikasso, Ségou and Gao. Wherever we went, people received us warmly and appreciated our music. We buckled down to the task of educating the masses. We had to make them understand that a visually impaired person needs to be treated the same as a person who can see. We gave talks before the concerts. We stressed the fact that pity should not be the only thing you feel for a blind person.

When we got back, Idrissa had found a solution to my problem with Mariam. With my help, he was going to organise a dancing party at his house. We made all the preparations and invited everybody we knew. We rented chairs, but there weren't enough. The house was full to bursting. There were two sheep on the spit, masses of drink, dessert. Idrissa whispered to me that God must favour this union since the evening was such a success. I made a speech in which I thanked everyone, including Mariam. I danced with her quite a few times. I finally told her, 'Mariam, I want you to know that I really fancy you and I...' but my voice trailed off. After a short silence, she replied, 'Me too, Amadou, I really fancy you.' And she kissed me right there and then. I felt the doors of paradise opening.

Two days later, taking my brothers and sisters back to the station, I told my sister Djaba about Mariam. She said, 'I find her very nice and, listening to her, she certainly has talent. But you're both disabled. You'll be entirely dependent on sighted people. It's a problem. I only want what's best for you.' Afterwards I thought about what my sister had said, but there was no question of me giving up Mariam.

Not long afterwards, I received a letter from my parents announcing their arrival in Bamako. I understood that my sister had told them of our conversation. They were probably worried. My uncle was upset about not being in the picture about my romance with Mariam. His only question was whether she had agreed to marry me. He said my parents would be reassured if they could see I had the backing of the institute. We only needed to talk to them.

The conversation with my uncle was a bit of a comfort, but I wasn't as convinced as he was. I hate arguments and I hoped with all my heart that things would work out in peace and harmony. While I waited for my parents' visit, I introduced Mariam to my uncle. He had seen her several times on stage, but they had never spoken. He liked her, she seemed to him an honest woman. So he was ready to help me convince my parents. At the institute, Monsieur Konaté was also happy to plead my cause.

They finally arrived on a Wednesday. My father approached the subject by saying that I was still too young to take such decisions for myself. He added that he knew of my marriage plans and had come to let me know his opinion. He said to my uncle, 'We can't force him to do anything. The days when parents arranged marriages without their children's consent are over. If we are good parents, we should be concerned for Amadou and we should also be concerned for Mariam. Amadou sees only the present, it's up to us to see the future for him. He has managed to overcome his disability and he's doing really well, but what about the future? We know how precarious life is, things can change from one day to the next.'

My uncle's reply to this was a good one. He stressed that it was impossible to protect children from every eventuality, that there were no guarantees in life. Everybody had an opinion on the subject. Monsieur Konaté was very good. He was reassuring about what it was to live as a blind person. And he said very complimentary things about Mariam. He told my father that our relationship was logical. He understood my parents' anxieties and promised to support us as much as he could. He promised to make sure we learned Braille so we could stand on our own two feet. He pointed out that the institute took care of all its pupils' medical expenses and had its own dispensary. He finished by saying that he was sure Mariam and I would succeed in everything we did and that one day we might even join the staff of the institute.

My father finally conceded. He would let us get married. He seemed to think it was God's will. He had asked my mother's opinion, and she had approved. She asked a pile of questions about my future wife. She wanted to know everything. I wasn't able to satisfy her curiosity completely. I told her what I knew.

'She is rich because she has a share of an inheritance. She looks after all the girls in the institute, especially those who are blind, deaf and dumb. I also know she comes from a very good family and that her mother is still alive. Her father, however, died recently.'

My mother also asked how we'd manage if Mariam got pregnant and what would happen if no one was with us at the birth. I was well aware we'd always have to have someone with us. We could afford it, we didn't have money problems, thank God. My mother was proud that I could already keep myself whereas most young people my age still hadn't reached that stage. She wanted to bless our union.

'God willing you'll get along well together.'

'Amen.'

'God willing no one of bad faith will come between you.'

'Amen.'

'God willing you'll be spared misunderstandings and disappointments.'

'Amen.'

'God willing you'll have many children.'

'Amen.'

'God willing you'll have good health and success in whatever you do.'

'Amen.'

My mother's blessing reassured me, and I was happy. The discussion turned to politics. The military government was not fulfilling its promises. According to some, we were on the verge of anarchy. Others had visionary powers, but the situation wasn't at all clear. We went on arguing until dinner. Then someone shouted, 'Ceasefire, it's time to eat. You all know that an empty bag doesn't stand on its own. Cooking is a more ancient art than politics, and even music. Our ancestors don't like us talking too much while we're eating.' I accompanied Idrissa and Monsieur Konaté to the door since they wanted to take their leave. My uncle was with us, he whispered in my ear, 'You see, it all turned out all right in the end.' I thanked him.

Obviously I told Mariam everything that had happened when I next bumped into her at the institute. She said she'd told one of her sisters about me and suggested she meet my parents. She explained what she was planning to do.

'I'll go to the market and buy two chickens that I'll prepare with a *yassa* sauce.'

'Stop, you're making my mouth water…'

'Don't worry. I'll make enough for you to eat your fill as well.'

'When will all that happen?'

'Next Wednesday. My two sisters will help me.'

'Thank you, Mariam. It's important you meet my parents. What should I make for yours?'

'You're crazy. You're not a woman, you can't cook for my parents.'

'I know, just teasing you…'

I explained that my mother was very curious and wanted to know things about her that I didn't know myself. She told me to listen, she was going to tell me about her life.

Chapter Fourteen
Mariam's Story

'You don't need me to tell you my name and surname. My father was called Augustín Doumbia and my mother Kadiatou Dem. My mother had ten children, two died. I was born on 15 April, 1958, at Bamako. I'm the fifth child. My father married three women. The first was called Constance Traoré. My mother is the second. The third is called Oumou Doumbia, we call her Ba-Oumou out of respect, that means Mother Oumou. The other women also had children. So you can imagine how many children we have in our family. My family history must be very different from yours.

My father and my mother belonged to different religions. He was Christian, she was Muslim. Their marriage posed problems on my mother's side because my grandfather was an imam. The mosque's council insisted that my father Augustín Doumbia convert to Islam. He changed his name to Moussa. That's why I'm called Mariam.

The Ministry of Health and Social Services had only just been created and it wasn't as efficient as it is today – Mali had become independent only two years after I was born. The Malian state didn't have the means to prevent certain infant illnesses and vaccines weren't available for everyone. So I got measles. I was so ill that a lot of people thought I wouldn't survive. After the illness, I had bad headaches which later turned out to be eye-ache. I was five, but my eyes had been infected for some time. I lost ninety per cent of my vision. I can't see anything, but at certain times of the day I can vaguely see very bright colours.

In President Keïta's time, my father was a ministerial adviser. After that he became a headmaster and head of the parents' association. My family supported me throughout my disability. My father was particularly fond of me. He let me have everything I wanted and spoiled me. And I already took pleasure in looking after others in my family. Now I'm the president of our group of girls, the Noblewomen. There is Awa Djan Doumbia, whom we call Chimène (in Bambara the suffix *djan* means big), Diaminatou N'Gnang known as Charlotte, Awa Tall known as Ivon, Saly Kanté known as Sylvie, Nènè Kanté, Saly's sister, known as Véronique. I also act as a sort of mediator, to maintain harmony in the group. If for instance two members of the group have problems, I get them together and make them remember the good times they've had. It works just as well for my men friends.

I've been blind since I was five, but I've never been discriminated against in any way. Before the institute was set up, I went to primary school. I used my hearing to learn a few elementary notions. My father's third wife was a teacher at the school La République, where my father was the headmaster. She adopted me. She did a lot for me. She even took me into class with her. I listened to the lessons and managed to remember them. One of the students wrote the lesson for the day in my exercise book and, when I got home at night, one of my brothers or sisters would read them over a few times for me so I could remember them. That's how I got the little bit of education I have today.

My interest in music came later. Here in Bamako, the young lads in the neighbourhoods get together in groups, or what we call *grains*. The girls do the same, but theirs are more structured. We all contribute to a fund and, when we have enough money, we organise dance parties and invite everyone we know. My interest in music came when I began listening to a radio my father had. I was my father and mother's treasured child. Because I couldn't see, my father would lend me his radio, so I wouldn't be bored. As a kid, I liked French music, I was a fan of Sheila, Sylvie Vartan, Johnny Hallyday, Nana Mouskouri, Dalida and lots of other singers.

In those days, in our neighbourhood of Madiné-Koura, there wasn't enough electricity for street-lighting and lights in public places. We waited for the moon to shine so we could go out into the street and organise what in Bambara we call *têkêrê-tlolonguai*, "having fun by clapping hands". The girls would make a big circle, or a little one depending on how many we were, and we'd take turns dancing in the middle. On these occasions, I'd sing every song that came into my head: folk songs, pop songs, anything. My friends would clap their hands with me. That's how I became the mainstay of the group. When I wasn't there, the girls in my neighbourhood would stop playing. When there was no moon, we'd get together at somebody's house to tell stories and play guessing games. My parents encouraged me to sing. That's why my father lent me his radio. He hoped I'd be able to do it for a living.

At primary school, at home time, the teacher would ask me to stand in front of the class and sing. The other children would clap their hands or join in the song. I got to like singing so much that my classmates nicknamed me "Sheila" after the famous French singer.

When the institute was set up, my father's closest friend, Monsieur Diarra, who everyone in Bamako called Diarra No 2, got me an introduction. It's thanks to him and Tanti that I was able to enrol in the institute. At first, Uncle Dougoufana had his reservations. (Uncle Dougoufana was my father's eldest brother and it was he who later took responsibility for us after my father's death.) He was afraid I'd be an object of pity, a figure of fun. Diarra No 2 and his wife Tanti Renée insisted. To convince my uncle, they stressed the advantages the school could give me. They told him I'd learn Braille and I'd have the chance to better myself by learning to read and write. Unlike you, I'd never really had any education. Schools were only organised around children who could see, I had only been there to listen. They also said the institute could help me take up a musical career. My uncle finally agreed and handed over my birth certificate. That's how I enrolled in the IJA. I love music and I'd love to do it professionally in the future.

Your mother probably wants to know if I'm good at domestic chores. My mother had servants, and anyway, I was spared housework because I was blind. In Mali, cooking is all done on a wood stove and my eyes are very sensitive to smoke. All the same, when I was little I used to hang around the servants so I could learn what they did. On Sundays, I'd wash the clothes with them. I'd fetch water from the well, even though I was forbidden to. I forced myself to learn household things because I don't like being dependent. I promise you that, in the future, I won't expect a maid to replace me completely. I'll do things with her and do my part.

As far as your mother's last question goes: whether or not I want to have children. Yes, of course I want to. I don't know any woman who doesn't. My only condition is that the man I have children with spends the rest of his life with me. Also, I hope to marry a man who does not object to my making music.'

We went on to talk about music. She told me how much music meant to her, and I told her how much it meant to me.

'I can't remember a single week of my life when I haven't played music, at least in my head. For me, music is moral support but also a means of expressing myself, of dialogue with the world outside.'

'When we met, I especially loved the lyrics of your song "Dana-Môgô" Where do you get your inspiration from?'

'From listening to French songs. And you?'

'By listening to silence.'

At the institute, although most of the students were blind, they were all party to the news 'Amadou and Mariam are getting married'. It made us laugh because we weren't planning on getting married straight away.

When Wednesday afternoon came, my aunt asked me if I was nervous. I admitted I was. She told me to go and get ready because Mariam and her sisters would soon be here. I was in my room changing when I heard the voices of three young girls. My aunt told me discreetly that Mariam was very beautiful and was wearing a lovely embroidered *boubou*. I said my stomach was tortured by the fantastic smell coming from the kitchen. The meal was very good and the conversation pleasant. Mariam didn't say very much, but my mother liked her, so much so that she made a present of a silver bracelet.

My mother praised Mariam's beauty and said she was sure the first child would be a boy. She had the gift of second sight. Everyone was very positive. I didn't need to ask my father his opinion to know it. The evening before they left, Mariam returned with presents of cloth and jewellery for my sisters. She talked more than on their first meeting. I was so happy that I took her in my arms and hugged her. Normally in Mali, it's not done to embrace in front of your parents. I informed my parents that I was soon to meet all Mariam's family too. They gave me strict instructions as to what I should and should not do. It was mainly advice about good manners.

After Mariam had been to my home, we became even closer. There were fewer barriers between us, we were less reserved. Even the quality of our work improved. When new lyrics came into her head, she sang them to me and I tried to pick out melodies on my guitar to go with them. We composed a dozen or so songs like that. During breaks in lessons at the institute, she'd take her stick and come over to me, or I'd go over to her. We were so close some students started calling us 'the twins'.

The Wednesday of the meeting at Mariam's house, I spruced myself up. Following my uncle's advice, I wore traditional clothes. When Idrissa Soumaoro saw me, he whistled and laughingly called me 'Monsieur' in a respectful tone. The sun had already set when my uncle settled us into his embassy car. He coached us to first greet the elderly relatives, then the adults, and then the youngsters. I behaved as soberly as possible. I said as little as possible, replying yes or no. We stayed about an hour and a half then politely asked the way home.

By our respective visits, Mariam and I showed that we loved each other and that our intentions were serious. At the institute, rumour had it that we wanted to leave Eclipse and the school. It wasn't true but it didn't help our relationship with the rest of the band. The problem also was that we wanted to keep our own compositions. Our songs with solo guitar were very successful. It was true also that our work with the group brought us less and less money. People wanted to see the two of us rather than the band. They liked the traditional side of our creations.

I talked the problem over with Idrissa who understood but couldn't help himself repeating ad nauseam, 'I was one of the founders of Eclipse. I won't say a word against the band. You don't destroy what you created.' A couple of days later, the National Lottery contacted the institute to ask if we would write a song for the show, and if Mariam and I would perform on the night of the draw. The director of the institute wanted to discuss the internal conflict in the band which he thought was harming its development. He was unhappy about the turn things had taken. He was cross with those who had spread lies. He didn't even want to hear their side. We had a meeting and decided to expel the guilty parties.

Mariam and I had been astonished when Monsieur Konaté asked us to pay the institute for borrowing their amplifiers. He proposed a fee: twenty-five thousand CFA francs per amplifier. During the night, the lottery song came to me and I sang it to Mariam:

La loterie nationale du Mali.	Mali National Lottery.
Loterie nationale,	National Lottery,
Loterie est une bonne chose,	A lottery is a good thing,
Prenez les billets de la loterie nationale.	Get tickets for the National Lottery.
Si la chance vous sourit,	If luck smiles on you,
vous serez millionaire.	you'll be a millionaire.

Mariam sang it a few times until it took shape, then we tried out melodies till we found one that worked well. We sang it for Monsieur Konaté who, without more ado, got in touch with the Lottery personnel manager. We went straight to the studio to record it. When the jingle was played on Mali national radio, a lot of Malians really liked it, even those who didn't understand French. The Lottery suggested sponsoring a concert for us. We chose Malian National Armed Forces Day. It was called 'Lottery Evening with Amadou and Mariam'. We rehearsed a programme of eight songs with solo guitar. Two days prior to the concert, all the tickets were sold out. We were a bit nervous before the concert because of the great responsibility we'd taken upon ourselves. When you play in a band and the evening's a flop, you can blame the whole band. But there we were, just the two of us, taking all the risks alone. I told Mariam we had to give it everything we had. She agreed.

And that's exactly what we did. We played as if our lives depended on it. Although we couldn't see the audience, we sensed a wave of emotion that warmed our hearts. After the concert, our wallet swelled with two hundred thousand Malian francs, plus extras from the fans. The following day, we gave fifty thousand francs to the institute as we had agreed with Monsieur Konaté. Mariam suggested we save the money to buy our own amplifier. People who were at the concert and knew we studied at the institute came by to congratulate us. Some came with cameras. Others gave us money. Some members of Eclipse said they were proud to have us in the band.

The following day, Monsieur Konaté had a visit from two journalists from Mali National Radio who wanted to interview us and take pictures for the newspapers. The success of the Lottery concert marked the beginning of a career for Mariam and myself, a career that would have its highs and lows.

A couple of days later, Mariam said she needed to talk to me. I asked if it was about Eclipse, she said no. I asked if it was about the institute, she said no. I asked if it was about the concert, she said no. When finally I asked if it was about her family, she didn't reply. So I took her under the big mango tree and we sat down. There, Mariam told me that her mother's family opposed our union. She added, 'I'm worried because they want to persuade my mother not to agree. My uncle is educated, for him the most important thing is the love that unites us. But the others are against us. They think our union has no future and that it would be better for each of us to marry people who can see. Marriage between two blind people brings too many problems.' It was the same argument my parents had used. Mariam went on, 'I don't think my mother can say no, and if she did, I'd do everything to make her change her mind. But I really would like my mother's respect and blessing.' I told her not to worry because I'd heard similar things at my house but they had done an about-turn. I assured her we would find a solution, that my uncle would talk to her mother.

I waited until the weekend to discuss it with my uncle. He said he understood Mariam's anxiety and advised me to get engaged quickly and start living together. He explained, 'You could rent an apartment in Bamako to begin with. I'll help you move. If your parents and Mariam's family see that you can live together with no problem, they'll finally be convinced there's no reason why you can't get married.' He went on to tell me that he himself had also had trouble being accepted into my family. He was a bit of a hippy and they didn't like that. So he and my aunt had had to hide things from them. Mariam and I agreed we had to follow the procedures of a traditional Malian marriage.

Chapter Fifteen
Nuptials

My uncle explained that the ceremonies involved in a marriage came in three stages. There was the role of the *griot* and the gift of seven *kola* nuts, then later a hundred kilos of *kola* nuts to be shared among my wife's family and friends. The money I was able to put in the pot was meagre because I didn't earn a massive amount. It was just enough to buy clothes, cigarettes, tea, etc. I had certain disadvantages in the eyes of my family-in-law: I was poor, blind, and had already made their daughter pregnant. I had, as they say, 'put the cart before the horse'.

On the bright side, however, I was following the stages of a traditional marriage to the letter. I chose a *griot* who brought Mariam's uncle the *kola* nuts (her father being deceased). He had to accept them, of course, if I were to have a chance of marrying Mariam. I was terrified of this moment. What's more, Kabinet, the *griot*, took his time returning from his mission. My uncle smoked cigarette after cigarette. In the end, Kabinet came back all smiles saying that he had talked to Mariam's uncle about her father, a very good man. Kabinet added, 'We *griots* have a saying: it's the empty barrels that make most noise.' Wise men keep their counsel. We then discussed the situation in Mali and he bemoaned the state of the country.

In Mali, it's the *griots* who pass stories down the generations. They are distinguished from other tribes by their surnames: Kouyaté, Diabaté, Keïta, Demba... They know the history of every family, every tribe, and the wars that pitted one against another. They are the guarantors of good human relationships and respect for traditions. They are living libraries. You can only criticise *griots* for four things: if they're not good talkers, if they don't sing, if they don't play an instrument, or are not discreet. For *griots*, proverbs make words binding. My uncle took this opportunity to sound out Kabinet. Could we move things on a bit faster? He said it shouldn't be a problem, that's what he was there to facilitate. We stayed chatting until the heat went out of the sun.

The wedding date was set.

One Monday morning, my uncle smirked and said he would gladly help me choose my best clothes so that I'd be handsome for Mariam.

'But Uncle, don't forget Mariam can't see me.'

'She can't see you but she'll hear from the teachers and other people at the institute that you have made yourself very handsome for her. True or false?'

'You're right, I hadn't thought of that.'

So I spruced myself up and listened at the door for the noise of a car engine. Monsieur Konaté arrived in buoyant mood and said, 'Mr President, Your Excellency Monsieur Bagayogo, allow us the pleasure of requesting you take your seat in this new bus temporarily fitted out for you while your Rolls Royce is being cleaned.'

We burst out laughing. We went round picking up the students one by one. Around 8 o'clock, before classes started, the bus dropped us off in the schoolyard. I managed to get a moment alone with Mariam and she confirmed with great joy that the *griot's* tactics had almost done the trick. Her mother was nearly convinced. Mariam had undergone gruelling questioning about me, and her feelings for me. She told me in great detail what had gone on in her family and what they had said.

Then we discussed more concrete things, like the furniture we needed to buy, all the expenses we had to cover. We went over our plans until the first bell rang and we each went into our class. My thoughts were chasing each other around my head. I had too many things to sort out, but I was very contented. When I assessed my time spent at the institute, the result was very favourable. I could read Braille and I could even teach it. The director had actually suggested I become a teacher there because the number of students kept increasing. I would get paid for it, and have my own classes at the same time. The situation was only temporary, the time it took for the director to find qualified teachers.

One day, Mariam arrived at our house with two of her sisters. We were drinking Malian tea. My uncle and aunt were delighted to see her. She thanked my uncle for Kabinet's intervention, and said that was the reason for her visit. We laughed a lot because Mariam's sisters started imitating Kabinet. When they had left, I revelled in the situation. That night my uncle told me about a house we might be able to rent thanks to a colleague of his, another chauffeur at the Czechoslovakian embassy. He also knew of a carpenter who could sell us some furniture. We should be able to manage. Between our two teachers' salaries and various concerts we were giving, it was feasible. Mariam wanted her mother to help us but I wasn't keen. When I saw we weren't in agreement, I preferred to give in.

She and I both counted the days. The following Saturday, as the sun went down, we waited with my uncle for Kabinet to come. As he got out of the taxi, he started singing 'Soliwo' in Bambara:

A yé na ka li yé
So ni na yé
Si ri ga lii yée
Fa dou ga dia bira
Ba dou ga dia bira

The neighbours all came running to listen to him. Without even asking if his mission was accomplished, my uncle ran to fetch his guitar. Kabinet began his performance: 'A sauce can be eaten without salt, but it tastes better with it.' The party started. Kabinet sang the praises of the Bagayogo, my family, and the Diarra, for Uncle Madou. He went through our whole history, the difficult battles our kings had fought against the colonisers and the other tribes in Africa.

I had tears in my eyes, I felt so emotional. He added that our ancestors preferred death to slavery. He also saluted our ancestors lying in the ancient cemeteries, 'there where weakness no longer says yes, there where pride no longer says no, there where hope no longer torments us mortals.'

Afterwards, he recounted what had happened at Mariam's house. Her family had consented. We thanked him warmly for his skill. After he'd left, we continued our discussion. My uncle didn't want Mariam's family to help us financially either. He was afraid she might reproach me for it one day, if by any chance there were problems between us. He was right because anything could change. He made me promise to convince Mariam that we shouldn't begin our married life with cash from her family.

That week, Idrissa had brought us newspapers which had articles about Mariam and me. He said the photos were very good but the articles were mediocre. He said journalists always tried to appeal to their readers' compassion and highlight the fact we were blind rather than the fact that we were good musicians. I knew they did it to sell their miserable rags. My uncle read the articles out loud. He added that, on the contrary, he thought it was all very favourable.

Mariam and I had started teaching. Me, Braille and she, dyeing techniques. It was all very new for me. I was excited and I think my pupils were too. I started by talking about who I was, my life, my music, Mariam. Some of them already knew. Then, I told them to stand up one by one and introduce themselves, as I had done. When the atmosphere was more relaxed, we began the lesson. I got a lot of pleasure from it because it made me feel useful. When the bell rang, I went to find Mariam and she said she'd felt the same pleasure.

The following week was very busy because the newspaper articles had had their effect. Offers of concerts flowed in. We gave two: in a cinema and once more in the former soldiers' hall. We again tried to present the Eclipse band rather than our duo, but it didn't work. With the teaching and studying timetable at the institute, we only had weekends and days off for performances. Monsieur Konaté helped print the tickets for our next show. They said 'Amadou and Mariam in Concert'. This time, there were not only press cameras but TV cameras too. The show lasted two hours and it was an amazing success. We earned 150,000 Malian francs each.

We went to visit the house my uncle had found. It was near the institute and the price was affordable. You could hear birds singing. There was a terrace and a veranda connecting the four rooms. The house didn't have the modern toilets I got used to later in life, it just had a hole. Using my hands and feet, I touched everything the agent showed us. In the courtyard was a deep well. I asked my uncle to decide for us. He took a deep breath and announced he accepted the offer.

He thought we would be happy in that house because the rooms were vast and very light, the courtyard would help us escape the heat of the night, and the proximity to the institute was a huge advantage. Besides, the price was reasonable. My uncle handed me the keys and I told myself that all I had to do now was arrange a date for the move with Mariam. She trusted me. As long as I liked the house, she said, she'd be happy to go and live there with me. As far as she was concerned, we had the same interests, so our tastes should be the same. She also said it seemed like a good deal.

Our recent success with the weekend concerts pushed up demand even further. Certain organisers were ready to pay more when we let it be known we weren't available. Among the offers, was one from an NGO. I promised to talk to Mariam about it. We were so overwhelmed by work, it was hard to imagine we'd be free to play the following weekend. Mariam wasn't keen but she agreed to talk to them, it was an NGO that combated eye disease. They wanted us to help warn people about it through the dance parties they organised. There was one the following Saturday.

We already had a gig. But they insisted and suggested the following weekend. Mariam finally said yes, so I accepted. Women are always in the driving seat. What woman wants, God wants! Besides, we really hit if off with that NGO.

I thought we'd be overwhelmed in the days ahead. All the same, I was pleased by the insistence of the NGO and the numerous concert offers. It was all very promising. But my students were worried because they said I would stop teaching them when I was a star. I began making mistakes in class because I was so distracted. I couldn't concentrate.

I was worried because on the one hand, I was delighted our career was taking off, but on the other I couldn't bear, and didn't understand, the obligations that came with it. Talking it over with Mariam, we agreed we needed to write more songs so our public wouldn't get tired of us.

My uncle had received a letter from my parents. They too increasingly favoured my union with Mariam, but they insisted we respect tradition. This meant we had to wait to get married, and especially be married before we moved in together. The letter also mentioned that my father was ill. He had problems with his lungs, he had had to give up smoking. My uncle left me alone to think things over. I was very worried. I didn't know how to reconcile all these contradictions. Later on, we brewed some tea together and discussed everything. I finally decided I needed to visit them.

As it happened, Monsieur Doumbia had invited me to play in Koutiala with Mariam. That fitted in really well. At the same time, my students had spoken frankly to me about the decline in the quality of my teaching. I admitted I was having trouble coping with so many things on all fronts, but that things would improve.

We were leaving for Koutiala in the next three weeks. We told Monsieur Konaté we were going to get married and would have to withdraw from activities at the institute for a while. He enquired about Eclipse, and Mariam's troupe. I assured him this was a temporary situation and that we would help him find solutions. I'd already arranged for another teacher to take my students. But Monsieur Konaté was displeased that I had not warned him in advance. I realised my students had complained about my lack of concentration and I reprimanded them for this afterwards. I didn't appreciate them maligning me behind my back. One of them spoke up.

'We're eight students in this class. Rest assured half of them have absolutely nothing against you or Mariam, and that includes me. I'll tell you something you don't know, but should know. Rumour in the institute has it that Mariam and you are richer than anyone else here and it's time you helped the establishment financially. We're here because we all suffer from the same disability, we can't see. Our disability is the same, but our futures are different. A minority wanted to talk to Monsieur Konaté. We're sorry. Some of us didn't agree with this approach, or didn't even know. That's all I wanted to say. Thank you.'

In fact it was me that should have been thanking him for reassuring me about the number of students in the class who were hostile, and telling me about the growing jealousy in the institute. I read somewhere in a Braille text that the eye doesn't see everything, but that the eyes are the windows of the soul. I told Mariam about the rumours.

We gave the concert for the NGO but I realised that Gilbert, the Canadian I dealt with, was misinformed about the cause of our blindness. He thought we had suffered from onchocerciasis, the disease his organisation was combating. When they realised their mistake, it didn't seem to bother them, they still wanted to do their campaign with us. I felt betrayed.

On the way home, I was exhausted. I was beginning to feel seriously fatigued. I should have got up early the next morning to give a lesson at the institute. But I couldn't. I needed to stay in bed. My aunt passed the news to the driver coming to fetch me, and to Mariam. When she heard, Mariam insisted on getting off the bus to come and see me. That day, a day that began in such a hum-drum fashion, was engraved in my memory. We spent the day just talking to each other. It was a beautiful day.

Chapter Sixteen
Perpetual Motion

Then the frenzy of activity began again. We taught lessons on Mondays and Tuesdays, we gave concerts on Saturdays and sometimes Sundays. Mariam's family agreed to let her come with me to do the concert in Koutiala and get to know the rest of my family. Even though we were adults, we always had to ask our parents' permission for everything. We began preparing for the journey. Mariam bought gold and silver jewellery, and very pretty expensive locally-made cloth for my mother and sisters. For my brothers, she bought jeans that the tailors in Bamako sewed and sold in the market. For my father, she found anti-pneumonia medicine. I don't think her shopping list forgot anybody. I had the feeling I'd known Mariam for an eternity and that my life would have no meaning without her.

It was rare for a day to go by in Bamako without hearing one of our songs on the radio. Our duo had become very famous. When we had finished all our preparations, including the repertoire we were going to play in Koutiala, we fixed the departure date. We went by car. I only brought two guitars – acoustic and electric – and I persuaded Mariam not to borrow the institute's amplifiers which cost us too much money.

Having a telephone was rare in those days, so we couldn't warn my family of our arrival. It was a huge surprise. My parents welcomed me as if I were the Prodigal Son. My sisters got my room ready and we soon felt very much at home. My sisters stuck to Mariam like glue. They took her to the toilet, joked with her, cooked with her. I embraced my parents. I sensed my father wasn't well. He didn't join in the conversation and complained about a pain in his chest. His voice was weak. My mother said he spent most of the day lying down. As an exception, he sat down and greeted us, and then went to lie down on his bed again. The state of his health was very worrying. The time came for present giving. They were all very happy. Small presents cement friendships.

Monsieur Doumbia came to the house to find me. He almost fell into my arms. He greeted Mariam with the same warmth, and ended by saying that words couldn't describe his happiness. He didn't talk about Koulistar. He no longer worked for the council officially but he used his experience in the music world to rent venues and organise concerts. I was dying to ask for news of Ouatt and all the others, but I followed the gist of his conversation.

Then he began telling us about the programme he had planned for Mariam and me. He said the first concert would be in Koutiala, then we would go to two other towns nearby, before returning to Koutiala for the last concert. He said he had all the technical backup we needed, and that we'd be paid according to the box-office takings.

Talking to some of the fans later, I finally found out that Koulistar was dead. One night, after a concert, some unknown person had forced the door of the shop where the group kept their instruments. The most expensive had disappeared. Suspicion fell on Monsieur Doumbia, who was interviewed several times by the police and finally dismissed from his position. The whole town was talking about me and the concert we were going to give. Mariam was less fêted than me, because this was the town I had grown up in musically.

An incident took place on the evening of the concert. The security guards were overwhelmed then completely disappeared, leaving us at the mercy of a hundred delirious fans who wouldn't let us perform. Some of them mobilised to protect the stage but we were forced to abandon the concert. The next day, Monsieur Doumbia gave us 75,000 francs each. It was the lowest fee we'd ever received for a concert. We were astonished, but Monsieur Doumbia explained that someone had taken advantage of the chaos and raided the till.

As agreed, he came to get us in the morning to drive us to Kolondièba and Bougouni where we had another sell-out concert. Again Monsieur Doumbia gave us 75,000 francs each, this time on the pretext that the tickets had been hijacked. We found this hard to believe and refused to honour the last concert scheduled for Koutiala. He tried to persuade us to do the gig, but in vain.

We knew my uncle had delivered the second *kola* nut, and then the third, to Mariam's family. All that was left for her to become my wife, were the religious and civil weddings according to the ancient laws of Mali. I gave my uncle the appropriate money for him to do the necessary for the two ceremonies. Some friends of his helped me prepare the home we were moving to. I'd often heard the saying 'Good friends are worth more than bad brothers'. Offers of concerts kept raining in. We ended up playing not every weekend but every other day. We managed to pay off all the loans we'd had to take out. The dates for the religious and civil weddings were fixed.

My brothers and sisters came from Koutiala. My friends and colleagues, my uncle's friends and colleagues, Mariam's family and friends, and loads of other people, all gathered at the mosque in the evening. Throughout the night, the Christians read from the New Testament and the Muslims from the Koran the appropriate marriage verses. We stayed in the mosque until the cock crowed and the imam finally declared an end to the ceremony. Many of the congregation came to wish us joy: 'May your union be blessed with health, success, many children and understanding.' 'Amen,' we replied. I must have shaken more than a hundred hands.

The following day, in the eyes of my religion I was a married man. But I still didn't have the right to take Mariam to my house. That would have risked ruining the post-nuptials week which in Bambara is called *kognon-so*, or the 'new wife's bedroom'. The bride and groom have to spend a week in an isolated room under a mosquito net. An old woman looks after them, and that includes providing aphrodisiac drinks and advice if need be. The bride must be a virgin when she enters the *kognon-so* and ideally comes out pregnant.

We chose to get married on a Sunday. Compared to the religious festival, the civil wedding is much longer and more expensive, especially for Mariam and her family. Mariam received many presents from her childhood friends, friends from later in life, and her family.

The day of the wedding, my uncle and his friends formed a procession with their cars, and greeted our arrival at the town hall with a concert of klaxons. The car we followed them in was a limousine, I'm told. I'll remember our exchange of vows with the mayor as long as I live.

'Monsieur Amadou Bagayogo?'

'Yes, Monsieur le Maire.'

'You cannot see, but I hope you can hear me.'

'Yes, I hear you, Monsieur le Maire.'

'Do you accept with all your heart Mademoiselle Mariam Doumbia as your wife according to the law of the land?'

'Yes, I do.'

'Mademoiselle Mariam Doumbia?'

'Yes, Monsieur le Maire.'

'You cannot see, but I hope you can hear me.'

'Yes, I hear you, Monsieur le Maire.'

'Do you accept with all your heart Monsieur Amadou Bagayogo as your husband according to the law of the land?'

'Yes, I do.'

'If you both accept, affirm your vows by signing the civil state registers, to validate them under the law.'

The mayor took our hands and placed them on the register where we had to sign. I was overcome with emotion. I relived my life as a blind person as if I were in a film. A mixture of joy and sadness came over me. I no longer knew whether to laugh or cry.

Before disappearing off on our post-nuptials week, we tried to honour all the concert commitments we had made. All the more so, because we needed the money. We began our honeymoon with the pleasant feeling of having been able to cover all our costs. I was now, in the eyes of Malian law, a married man, and therefore responsible. A few months later, Mariam gave birth to a little boy whom I named after my father: Ibrahima. In Mali it's usual to give your father's or mother's name to your child. We moved to Faladié, and Mariam's mother found us two young girls, Kadiatou Diokoka and Sitan Camara, whom we hired to help us.

They were like sisters to us and became a part of our household. They liked living with us so much that they stayed many years longer than planned. In Faladié, in the evening, we rehearsed old songs and tried out new ones. As we played, the courtyard filled with spectators and it gradually turned into a kind of repertoire dictated by our neighbours.

In Mali in those days, there was no proper mechanism for helping artists get known abroad. The few Malian artists who had reputations overseas had gone through Abidjan in Ivory Coast. I was not yet bold enough to believe in an international career. Subconsciously one of my father's proverbs stuck in the back of my mind: 'If a person aspires to one and he gets two, he'll naturally try to have three, then four…' I was wary of being greedy.

One evening, while Mariam and I were rehearsing in our courtyard, a man came in and introduced himself. He seemed very well informed about music, and said he was a Malian recently arrived from Ivory Coast. He told us that unfortunately our repertoire did not lend itself to an international career, but that we were on the right track and could be on the road to success. He proposed managing our concert tours, first in Mali and then abroad if all went well.

Even though Monsieur Bamoye Keïta made a good impression on us and seemed to know what he was talking about professionally, Mariam and I couldn't help being suspicious. We had had so many disappointments. All the same, we accepted his proposition after asking how he intended to remunerate us. There were two ways of making financial deals: either agreeing on a sum before the concert, or sharing the takings at the box office afterwards. We preferred the first solution because it seemed more reliable. We asked for 150,000 to 200,000 Malian francs per concert.

With Bamoye, we performed in many different areas of Bamako. Then we ventured out into numerous towns throughout Mali, including Koutiala where we had the joy of spending time with my sick father again. In Koutiala, Bamoye gave my father money out of his own pocket. I was very moved by the gesture. He soared in my esteem. From then on, I thought very highly of him and we trusted him.

One fine morning, my uncle woke us very early with a voice that sounded like someone who had been crying a lot. My father had gone to sleep the previous evening leaving a message for my mother: that he was proud of me and wished me luck. I felt as if my life had ended. My father was the man I had always been able to count on. I cried my eyes out, like a child.

I was to leave for the funeral in Koutiala the following morning. I spent the whole day receiving condolences from friends, family and musicians who had learned the bad news and had come to share my grief. They filled the courtyard of our house. The next day, Monsieur Konaté lent us the institute's bus for the journey. It left our house full. Despite its wide social mix, the population of Mali share the same pain, the same hopes, the same joy and the same misfortunes. The Christians read passages from the New Testament, the Muslims read the Old Testament. They all prayed that God Almighty would receive my father among the saints and his soul would rest in peace. After the funeral, the others went back to Bamako while Mariam and I stayed in Koutiala to be with my mother.

When we finally got home, we continued the concerts in Bamako and round Mali. I was now mother's sole financial support. My father's death had left an emotional void in our family; in addition he was the only person who brought money home.

Mariam thought it would be simpler if my family was nearer us, so we could help them. My uncle agreed. He looked for a big house where we could all live together. But Mariam and I were used to our house and our neighbourhood. It gave us a certain autonomy. So we asked the owner if we could stay in our house and extend it. He gave his permission.

My mother agreed to come and live with us. So we hired a removal van and went to collect my family and their belongings in Koutiala. My fans there came to see me and said how sorry they were that I'd gone to Bamako. I would have liked to stay in Koutiala but I wanted to take my music career further, and destiny dictated I had to go.

There were many helping hands in Bamako to settle my family in. My mother, brothers and sisters installed themselves comfortably in four newly built rooms. I felt reassured. It was as if I'd recovered the part of me that had stayed in Koutiala. The arrival of my family meant there was much more activity in our house. And the concert offers had increased so much that Mariam and I couldn't accept them all. We said no straight away to the ones that meant we had to travel outside Bamako.

At the same time, some of the teachers at the institute, musicians from our old group Eclipse with whom I'd stayed in contact, used to come round to our house to say hello, drink Malian tea and discuss the possibility of furthering our careers outside Mali. One day, after a performance at Fana, a town several kilometres from Bamako, on the road to Ségou, we met a man called Cheick Sadibou, who invited us to play in Burkina Faso. He suggested being our manager. We explained that we were already trying to get known outside Mali, particularly in Ivory Coast, and that someone was already taking care of things for us there. He said that didn't stop him representing us in Burkina Faso. We said we'd think about it, and eventually came to an understanding. We agreed to meet four months later. It was September 1982, the year our second son, Samou Bagayogo, was born.

A week after we met Cheick Sadibou, Monsieur Konaté suggested I take part in a competition for young artists organised by Radio France Internationale in Lomé, the capital of Togo. You had to sing a song in an African language accompanied by a single musical instrument. Monsieur Konaté took advantage of our meeting to discuss Eclipse with me. I told him what I had in mind: that we disband the group and reform it exclusively with blind youngsters from the institute. He listened and agreed. The new group succeeded where the old one had failed.

I didn't feel guilty about leaving Mariam with the children because it's not a problem in Africa. There is always plenty of family around to help out. I was more anxious about my choice of song. Mariam advised me to sing 'Dounouya'.

So I left for Togo. It was the first time I'd been alone since our wedding day.

Chapter Seventeen
Around the World

When I got to Togo, I realised that the most important thing wasn't that I won. More interesting was taking part in the event, meeting other artists, and having the chance to make contacts that might get me access to an international career. We were about twenty artists in the competition.

One morning, when I was on the beach with some other musicians, I started rehearsing my song. Someone put a palm leaf beside me. As I played, I heard the sound of coins piling up on the leaf. People started talking about me in Lomé. It was the fourth day of the competition. Restaurant and bar owners asked me to come and play for them. The press wrote about me. I gave interviews in which I spoke on behalf of disabled people, and tried to transmit a message. I was criticised for not being more political. But I found politics dangerous because I didn't understand it totally. I preferred talking about a cause I was familiar with.

I was invited to the house of my friend Mamadou Kouyaté, who had emigrated here. I spent a wonderful evening with him. He was delighted to see me taking part in the competition. Malians are never short of things to talk about when they meet outside their borders. While we talked, the house gradually filled up with people who had learned via the bush telegraph that a Malian superstar and a blind youngster had got together. In the end, I had to leave his house under escort.

All this obviously influenced the jury. When I walked onto the stage, the audience applauded. The technicians came to adjust the mic and I began to sing 'Dounouya'. Some of the audience already knew it. Total hysteria followed. I finished the song and took a bow. When the results were read out, I was filled with joy. I had won. I jumped in the air and lots of people came to congratulate me. I thanked everybody and prayed the earth would weigh lightly on my father.

I had won a trophy and two million Central African francs. I was used to my music having followers, but I had never earned such a huge sum. I stayed another two days to do more interviews. The ambassador wanted to meet me. I was happy, but being away from Mariam cast a long shadow.

When I arrived back in Mali, fans waiting on the tarmac told me I was the pride of my country. I was pleased to have won a prize and money, and told myself it was good to be known in yet another African country. I gave part of the money to the institute. Mariam and I began planning our tour of Burkina Faso.

The tour was a disaster. We went to Bobo-Dioulasso and the concert proved catastrophic. The audience was very thin on the ground and most of the people there had managed to sneak in. We hardly earned anything. The other concerts followed a similar pattern. We had to send home for money. We realised our manager hadn't paid for the hotel which had been part of the original deal. The bill rose so steeply that we were forced to leave. Cheick Sadibou had disappeared into thin air. We never heard from him again, and the money I had earned in Lomé went up in smoke.

Mariam had the bright idea of asking Bamoye Keïta to come to our rescue. When he received our telegram, he came to pay our hotel and transport to Sikasso. We couldn't go straight back to Bamako. I sent my mother money and we stayed to play concerts in and around Sikasso. We were in great demand. Bamoye joked that we'd soon be in a position to buy our own aeroplane.

Bamoye was convinced we had to find someone who could help us market cassettes of our songs. He knew how to organise our concerts but hadn't a clue how to do all the rest. He gave us the address and phone number of a certain Ibrahima Camara, alias Calsso. He lived in Korhogo, on the border with Ivory Coast. We went to see him. We confided in him our dreams of branching out onto the international stage. He said he couldn't promise the international bit but he could arrange a tour of the area for us. We accepted.

After several performances, we had even more fans. We played to full houses all the time. Mariam and I were more than happy with our new life but we didn't abandon our plan to get ourselves known overseas. One day, Calsso mentioned a certain Adama Diarra who headed the *griots'* association in Abidjan. Many stars setting out on international careers had passed through his hands. He was originally from Mali and wanted to promote his country's music. Ask any taxi driver in Abidjan, they all knew him.

Mariam and I did a few more concerts in Ivory Coast, then decided to seek out Adama. We got to Abidjan and started our search. First we happened upon Sékou, then on Issa Dembèle, known as Issem, who said he would help us and offered to put us up. He in turn wanted to introduce us to a certain Kouassimi. We had long discussions with our new friends while we waited for him. He didn't show up until the following day, but we had a very good time with Issem in the meantime.

Kouassimi was a true professional. He suggested we make a video clip and said he'd help us promote our music. I had a cousin, Moussa, in Abidjan whom I phoned. He arranged concerts for us in the city and towns around, and got friends of his to organise the publicity. We filmed a video clip with Kouassimi around two of our songs. We loved the whole experience, filming in the countryside, on the beach...We started getting media coverage. God helped us realise our dream. We were beginning to be known outside Mali.

We took part in the programme 'African Stars', and this gave our career a further boost. The day after the programme, the hotel phones were jammed with calls for us. Issem and Sékou came over to tell us how proud they were to be our friends. We in turn thanked them for all their help. Shortly afterwards, Kouassimi brought a music producer originally from Nigeria to see us. His name was Aliou Maïkano. He was prepared to produce us, and put up the money himself. We agreed to work with him.

My cousin Moussa was taking care of the organisational side of the tours helped by a friend of his called Ismaïla Koné, alias Gordon Michel. Maïkano got us studio space in December 1988. The cassettes came out in March 1989. The first was in six parts and we called it *Amadou and Mariam, the Blind Couple from Mali. Volume 1.* Volume 2 followed a few months later. Maïkano was to take charge of the distribution and Issem would work with him. Our little music industry worked well and spread throughout Ivory Coast. We sold 25,000 copies of Volume 1. The business did well and we began making serious money, our first million Malian francs.

We became so well known in Abidjan that we were advised to hire two bodyguards to accompany us to concerts. We paid them according to the number of trips we made. It was during this period that we got the chance to meet the great Stevie Wonder. We had a jam session with him in our hotel room. He played the piano, I was on the guitar and Mariam sang. Playing music with him was very moving. We talked a bit despite the language barrier and he encouraged us a lot. He said he believed in us and that we had to persevere. It is a memory we treasure.

Maïkano also advised us to leave the hotel and move into a house. Everything was fine at home in Mali. After my father's death, my mother never missed a chance to tell me how much she missed me. Mariam received letters from her family saying the same thing. We missed them too. What's more, Mariam was pregnant with our third child, Kadiatou Bagayogo, who we had already nicknamed Tou, and she wanted to have the baby on Malian soil. And our album was coming out in Mali at the same time. So we decided to go back to Mali.

After our Malian visit, we returned to Burkina Faso where we got a rapturous welcome. From there, we continued on to Abidjan where Maïkano had begun recording Volumes 3, 4 and 5. He thought it best to bring them out in Bamako. But Sékou made the mistake of giving out complementary copies to journalists. These were copied like wildfire and we made nothing. Back in Bamako, everyone already had a copied cassette. That experience really hurt us. We were living on our savings and didn't know how we would repay Maïkano who had advanced all the money. We moved out of the rented house in Abidjan. Mariam lost a lot of sleep over it. Our hope that Abidjan would launch us internationally disappeared. We saw our departure from Ivory Coast as a failure. Our popularity hadn't really extended beyond the boundaries of the city. The desired explosion just hadn't happened.

We got out of this depressing mess by giving concerts in Sikasso and Ségou. And also because we received a miraculous telegram. It was from Sékou Minta, a Malian who lived in Paris. He had heard one of our cassettes and wanted us to play in his restaurant. He was willing to pay the airfare and our hotel. Before leaving for Paris, I settled matters in Abidjan and we held a big party with our friends in Bamako.

We arrived in Paris, and simply froze. Luckily Sékou Minta fed and clothed us. It was the second time I'd been to Paris, but you'd have thought it was the first. We made a deal with Sékou to play in his restaurant Farafina three times a week. A concert had also been organised in a hall in Saint-Denis. We were a bit disappointed because we'd very quickly realised we weren't known at all in Paris. We would have to win over audiences that were as yet indifferent.

Mariam and I redoubled our efforts, and taking a cue from Sékou, we managed to involve the audience in the performance by getting them to join in songs and repeat choruses, either in French or Bambara. It worked. Hope returned. One day, someone who had seen us in Bobo-Dioulasso came backstage. He wanted to help us. Meanwhile, we were receiving bills and worrying letters from Mali. The owner of our house threatened to evict the family if the rent wasn't paid. So we recorded an album in Paris. It was called *Wasso*, meaning Boasting, that had been released in Mali. Sékou Minta took charge of everything. We did some publicity, but our efforts hadn't been enough to reimburse him. So we sent cassettes to Mali to be sold through intermediaries.

Meanwhile, we played in the restaurant and did some concerts. The restaurant's clientele doubled thanks to us. But in the end we returned to Bamako with the feeling that our stay in Paris had not amounted to much. Before we left, a man handed us an envelope. Various Malians in Paris had clubbed together to help us. The 6,000 French francs in the envelope were enough to solve our problems in Bamako.

Back in Mali, we set off on a grand tour round the country. We went to Bla where we caused a riot. Mariam said that her mother was right to compare life to a pendulum that swings between happiness and misfortune, joy and sadness. The enthusiasm of the people here at home reassured us, all the more so because we had missed it in Paris. On the road to Tominian, we received a telegram from Mariam's sister telling us about a French guy, Marc-Antoine Moreau, who seemed keen to help us. He was in Mali and Mariam's sister had met him at a bus station. They'd started talking by chance and had got on to the subject of music. In the telegram, she said he worked as an artistic director in a big record company and was a fan of Malian music. He had heard one of our songs and wanted to meet us. Meeting Marc-Antoine was a decisive moment for us. He was, and still is, a very precious friend.

His intelligence and his modesty, despite the important things he had done, really impressed us. He also knew how to behave with disabled people. He wasn't in the slightest bit embarrassed. We talked about the possibility of him producing or remixing our album *À Chacun Son Problème* (To Each His Own Problem). Both Mariam and I were convinced that working with him would be a huge step forward for us and that we could travel a long road together. We've been travelling it for twelve years.

All the cassettes sent back to Mali had been sold. We hadn't told Sékou about Marc-Antoine, but we were in touch with him regularly and it became impossible to hide the fact that Marc-Antoine, who we had begun calling Marco, really wanted to take charge of our recording career. He opened negotiations with his record company while we were in Mali, and finally landed us a contract that he brought to Bamako for us to sign. The terms were good. Mariam and I would receive a sum of about 150,000 French francs, the equivalent of 15 million Malian francs.

Marco had reckoned on us arriving in Paris at the beginning of 1997. That coincided with a conference that Polygram had organised in London for all its musicians. That's how we met stars like Faudel and Yuri Buenaventura. And it was in London that Mathieu Chedid first captured our hearts. He has unfailingly supported us, played with us, and offered us opportunities like opening for him at Bercy.

He is generosity incarnate. When our record came out, we gave several concerts, one of them at the Flèche d'Or. We went on radio and TV.

A year later, in 1998, we were invited to the Transmusicales festival. We hadn't released an album in France at the time, but nearly a thousand people were in the audience. We were truly astonished. Everyone knew our song 'Je pense à toi' (I Think of You). We had to play it four times. Afterwards we were told that they don't usually do encores at the Transmusicales, so repeating it four times was... We were so delighted because you could hear the audience's enthusiasm. It was wonderful. At one stage, when we were singing 'Regardez cet homme, il est fatigué' (Look at that man, he's tired), the audience finished off our lines.

After the concert at Transmusicales, lots of journalists from France and other European countries began taking an interest in us. We gave interviews almost every day. We hoped it might help get us a production contract. We only had a recording contract. Polygram Jazz had signed us up, thanks to Marc-Antoine.

Since then, the Good Lord grants our every wish. We criss-cross a planet our eyes cannot see. We play all over the world. There are very few countries we haven't played in. All this fortune is not due only to our talent as musicians but most of all to the grace of God, and the indulgence and warm hearts of millions of people who help and appreciate us, those we call our fans.

Among the most important of our musical journeys

round the world was a concert we did in Brazil in 2001, when we were invited to a festival in Rio. Mariam and I were on stage and all around us was an audience in a state of total frenzy. The clamour of the crowd three hundred and sixty degrees around us was so overwhelming I nearly dropped my guitar. Nobody in Brazil knew us, and yet we were inspired by the love of this enormous crowd acclaiming us.

In 2004, we had an opportunity to work with Manu Chao, with whom we recorded the album *Dimanche à Bamako*, (Sunday in Bamako), which was a great success. We then made an album with the cooperation of musicians like Damon Albarn, who had involved us on a project of encounters, Africa Express.

Mariam and I are now asked to spread a message of peace and love via the universal language of our music. We want to continue doing this. We will go on fighting to help those who are in distress, especially blind people with whom we share our fate. At first, Mariam and I worried about the disadvantages our disability would bring. But over time, we became firmly convinced that it is not the Good Lord's way to give people everything.

If He makes you very tall,
you envy those who are smaller than you.
If He makes you very small,
you envy those who are taller.
If He makes you important and famous,
you envy those who aren't known at all and pass unnoticed.

This same Good Lord has lent us, here on earth, many things we would never have dared dream of. At the same time, He deprives us of the light of day. But even though we don't see our fans, we feel their sympathy. And we count on that sympathy to say to all disabled people, no matter what their disability, you mustn't let it stop you doing whatever it is you want to do.

In the hope that this book will inspire both those with disabilities and those without, Mariam and I would like to take this opportunity of saying to the world:

THANK YOU

Postscript
An Afternoon with Amadou and Mariam

It's December 2009 and Amadou and Mariam are sat in a London hotel on a damp and cold afternoon talking to Andy Morgan about their life and phenomenal global success. They are at the tail end of a long and intense period of gigging and promotional work. The night before the pair had blown away a packed house at the Forum, eliciting a passionate response from the diverse crowd of young indie kids and older African music lovers.

The day after the interview, Amadou and Mariam were due to meet other cultural ambassadors at a one-day conference organised by the cultural arm of a major sport-shoe manufacturer. The week after, the duo were due to fly to Oslo to shake hands with Barack Obama and perform at a special concert in his honour alongside Wyclef Jean, Donna Summer, Will Smith and other African diaspora glitteratti, at the Nobel Peace Prize award ceremony.

In the book you say 'We criss-cross a planet our eyes cannot see'. Do you enjoy travelling?

AMADOU: Yes, we love travelling because for us it is about being able to go to other places and meet other people. The magic of travelling is that every time we travel we find ourselves in the company of different people. And that appeals to me a lot, as a musician. When you go to a place that you don't know, the people there encounter you for the first time, so they're very interested, and you are too. It's all fascinating. You give the best you can give. It's not déjà vu, it's a new arrival.

You say that you almost paint a picture of a person in your head when you hear their voice, or shake their hand. Can you paint the picture of a city as well, through its ambiance, its smells, its sounds?

AMADOU: Yes, already just on the basis of the sounds of a city, you can create an image in your head. For example, when you arrive in Kinshasa, you know that the atmosphere is different to that of New York. You know it's different to the atmosphere of Paris. So you create this idea in your mind. You make a picture of the architecture, how the houses are built. Paris is a really really great place, which is well built, but the street map of Paris is like the street maps of the villages we have back home. You see? Because villages have this kind of shape [illustrates by snaking his hands round in spaghetti gestures]. You enter, and the streets go this way, that way and the other way. It's different to Bamako for example, which is all square. I was born in Bamako, so I know all the blocks of Balagajui, Hippodrome etc. I know that if you go that way you'll arrive there, and you can go on to that place. But in Paris, you mustn't do that. Going to Paris is like going to Djenne. When you go to Djenne, the streets are narrow, corridor-like and all jumbled up, so you get lost very quickly.

We've understood New York a bit, because it resembles Bamako in a way. These great big avenues and blocks. I'm already able to get an idea of the place. I'm in the habit of directing drivers to various places in Bamako, that I know well. So I know that once you've arrived at this level, then you must be here, or at that level, then you must be there. I know that.

During these trips, do you often suffer from homesickness?

AMADOU: Hmmm... yes. Often. Me, personally, what I miss is Malian tea and meat. I really like taking tea whilst eating meat. I really miss that when we're on tour. You can eat meat, but you don't have the right kind of tea with it. So, when I go to Mali I love drinking a glass of tea in one hand and eating meat with the other hand. I miss that a lot.

MARIAM: I often miss our local fish food, the 'Capitaine'. I really love that.

AMADOU: We also have a quality which is the ability to adapt to circumstances. As soon as I get back to Bamako, the first thing is... tea! But when we're in places where there's no tea, I can go for two months without drinking any. It's no problem for me.

When you were young, Bamako was a little village compared to how it is now. And also, Mali, like everywhere else in the world, has been subjected to accelerated modernisation. Do you sometimes feel nostalgic for how it used to be in your childhood?

AMADOU: Yes. When we were very young, we knew the neighbourhood. Almost all the locals knew each other, so there was that interconnection between people. The parents of your friends were also your parents. We had fun together. If there was this other child who was being naughty, there was another father who would come...

MARIAM: ...and tell everyone off. Nobody would dare answer back. And then when I was young too, we girls would go out in the moonlight to the river bank. We'd have fun out there. We'd sing. Nowadays they don't do that because of TV. So, really, it's disappeared. And then often when we were young, we'd go to each others houses and tell stories. Now they don't that. Everybody's just watching TV. It's not the same.

AMADOU: We remember, when we were young, there was the Marché de la Medina, the old market. It wasn't expensive. You could make tea. The charcoal sellers weren't far away. As kids we never used to buy the charcoal, we just used to pick up pieces that the sellers had dropped by mistake on the road. Ha ha ha.

MARIAM: And we used the same charcoal to cook with... It's really not the same now.

And the Institute for the Blind, is it still working well?

MARIAM: It's still there and we're still involved. There are people there, teachers, pupils, but, well... it's not like it was before.

AMADOU: It's become very big compared to what it was. Before, right at the beginning, there weren't many people. So the employees were always there for you. Now there are many people, and it just carries on. The structure has changed. Before it was only blind people, but now there's a kind of integration going on because, from Year 7 onwards, other sighted children from the neighbourhood come and enrol along with the pupils from the institute. So it's changed shape a bit, but it continues.

Has the attitude of the general populace towards the handicapped and the blind got better since you were young?

AMADOU: Yes. Before, the blind were marginalised and forced to beg. But now it's changed because we have blind people who are magistrates, we have blind people who...

MARIAM: ...are teachers. Others who are doctors. So it's got a whole lot better.

AMADOU: When we were at the institute we contributed a lot to that process. We wrote songs to raise awareness, and set up these open weeks of solidarity so that people could see our work. There are plenty of people who went to work at the institute thanks to the music we made. We transmitted plenty of messages and the joy of the kids was palpable, so it really motivated people.

Have the therapies and treatments available got better?

MARIAM: Yes, I think that medicine has progressed a lot since when we were young.

AMADOU: Now they manage to heal cataracts for example. But I think that in the old days, people were very kindly and affectionate in the way they dealt with you. There was a certain bond between doctor and patient. When we were hospitalised, we knew everyone, there was this bond which was woven between the patients themselves and the medical staff too.

Are you still in touch with all those musicians who played an important role at the start of your career?

MARIAM: Well, we're still in touch with certain musicians, like Idrissa Soumaoro. We're still in touch with him. And, well, there are also some musicians who have passed away so…

AMADOU: There's Zani Diabate. He's still around, playing the djembe and the guitar. He still has his band. So when we're in Bamako we play with them from time to time. It's a pleasure, a great pleasure for us. We also meet up with Traore Addès. We haven't lost touch completely.

Do you ever meet musicians from back home who say, 'Ah, it's really amazing what's happened!' having known you in the 1970s at the Institute and in the Ambassadors and all that, and now, when you're successful all over the world?

AMADOU: Yes, yes. It happens. They talk about that a lot. When they see us...

MARIAM: ...they congratulate us, they're proud of us.

AMADOU: Absolutely. In Mali, generally, people like to talk. They find themselves round at their friends, and they manage to talk about us, and when they listen to our music they say, 'Yes, we knew them way back when! Have you seen how they've taken off?' I think that maybe they never imagined that things would turn out like this. But I think they're very proud. It surprises them at times and it gives them hope too. I think that's what's most important.

Are there young people back home who think that you have the capacity too to give them opportunities and open doors for them? Do they come and see you to ask for help with their careers?

AMADOU: Yes, it happens all the time. To begin with, people asked us to find them labels and producers, things like that. But now people ask us to actually produce and release their music ourselves. So there are plenty of young musicians who wait for us with their cassettes and who want us to listen to their music. I think this is due to the fact that Mali is stuffed full of talent, but the music business there is deeply flawed because piracy has resulted in a lack of labels and royalties, so people put all their hope in an international career. That's why all these people come to see us and ask us to find them a label or an agent. Otherwise, back in the day when the system really worked and the scene was very active, these hopefuls went to see local producers and the cassettes were released and everything functioned well.

MARIAM: But thanks to piracy, everyone has just given up, really. It's hard to make cassettes now.

Has it occurred to you to maybe produce music yourselves, and set up a little studio in Bamako, or do that kind of thing?

MARIAM: Yes, there was a time when we were thinking seriously about that.

AMADOU: We're still thinking about it. Because, in fact, as an elder person who has reached a certain level, in our country, it's a kind of duty to help those coming up. If you manage to do something, and attain a certain success, you have to think of others too, and help them to climb the slope. So we've always thought of setting up a studio, maybe not immediately, but perhaps sometime soon we want to find the means to help people. Because at the moment, we're busy setting up the orchestra of the Institute of Young Blind Persons. So, we're on it. Our problem is that we're not in Mali an awful lot and that blocks us a bit.

You've played with all kinds of people but in your heads, do you still have dreams or desires to work with other people, with whom you haven't already played.

AMADOU: We've listened to so many people, and to so much music, that it's a bit hard to say. I don't think we're going to be able to play with all the people we'd like to play with. But on a human level, the encounters that really touched us were with David Gilmour... we never would have imagined that. But it happened! With Robert Plant too... we played with him, but just on the same bill. Not like David. We actually shared a stage with David, which was great. Stevie Wonder too. We met him in Ivory Coast and we sung together and to sing with him again would be wonderful. And we've always admired great artists like Francis Cabrel. The fact that we were also able to play with him in a TV programme was really really great. So, I think that essentially it's all about feeling, meeting people and discovering that you're heading in the same direction as them and that it's possible to do things together.

What have you learned from working with Manu Chao specifically, did that experience show you anything?

AMADOU: Well in fact when we met each other, it was a case of two different styles of music. So we put our trust in him to make the album. And what we learned was a way of singing, the harmonisation and the tendency to shorten the songs a bit. And also simplicity, digging out the essence of a song. That's very important.

How many children do you have now?

MARIAM: We have three children, two boys and a girl. The second boy, DJ Sam, sings, plays guitar and raps. He has a group called SMOD and his album will be released soon. He's been working with Manu Chao as well.

And you have grandchildren now too. What do you feel about that role?

MARIAM: Yes, it's beginning ha ha ha! Our first boy has had a girl, and she's called 'La Petite Mariam'. She's one year old. My daughter too has had a boy, not even a week ago. I find the role of grandparent really interesting because I like them to be near me and to look after them, to give them their bottle, their food. I really love it. And I have plenty of stories to tell them because, our parents, they told stories. They told us about many things.

So DJ Sam does hip hop, do you like that kind of music?

AMADOU: Yes, we like that music a lot. It's music for the young and they manage to communicate important messages. We also transmit messages, but not in the same way. Fundamentally it's the same thing. It's just the lifestyle that's different. And the fact that Sam has taken that route has given him a personality...

MARIAM: We encourage him... it's great.

Do you listen to lots of rap, or Malian rap, for pleasure?

AMADOU: I like listening to rap. When we first arrived in France I loved listening to rap. I listened to the messages, on Sky Rock, on plenty of other rap radios. I really liked Doc Gyneco. We listened to him a lot. And that other one too... Neg Marrons and MC Solaar who did 'Bouge de la'.

MARIAM: Well we like rappers that give out messages but not in a violent way.

AMADOU: There's this tendency to compare rappers with traditional *griots*. Maybe in terms of approach and structure, the way in which the *griots* speak, and rappers also speak, it's really there that the link exists. But the messages aren't the same. Because the *griots* are all about tradition, praise singing, and the rappers are about denunciations, about the stance, and that's it.

You've won plenty of prizes and you must have a lot of cups on the mantlepiece at home! Is there one set of laurels or one prize that is especially dear to your hearts, amongst all that you've won?

AMADOU: The Victoire de La Musique, yes...

MARIAM: It really meant a lot to us.

AMADOU: It's dear to our hearts. Because even when we were in Mali we used to listen to the broadcasts from the Victoire de la Musique awards ceremony. That really touched us. The difference is that the Victoire is awarded by professionals and for an African to receive a prize like that abroad, especially in Europe...

MARIAM: ...that's really something...

AMADOU: ...and it isn't something that's just idly given away. It really rewards some serious work. And that's what was very comforting. Well, because it's not given by Malians, it's given by the French, to an African...

MARIAM: ...it really gives you courage.

Next week you'll be taking part in the Nobel Peace Prize, which will be awarded to President Obama. What does being invited over there make you feel?

MARIAM: It's a pleasure to go there and sing in front of Obama. It's a real pleasure for us.

AMADOU: It's a very significant moment. When we were starting out as musicians in our country, and we went to Ivory Coast, well, we never imagined that we'd ever be invited to a ceremony in front of the President. So it's a recognition of our music and it's also a recognition of African music in general. It means that the work we're doing is beginning to be recognised and it can be wedded to other cultures and things in the world.

And is Obama someone who you admire?

MARIAM: Yes, he's someone we respect a lot. He's an African. When he was elected it made us very happy. Because he's an African, a black man, so when you have a President like that, it's a joy.

You're often spoken of as the ambassadors of Mali and Malian music, or even African music. What are the essential values of your country that you try and transmit and communicate when you're in Europe or the USA?

AMADOU: We are ambassadors and that's something that we wanted to become. We're very conscious of that role. In the case of Mali, the country acknowledges us as cultural ambassadors, who travel the world to talk about Mali, and reinforce the values of Malian music and culture in general. We've been decorated with the Chevalier de l'Ordre National by our government. So, because of that, we're very conscious of our mission.

Outside Mali, we try to make people aware that it is a welcoming country, which likes to look after people who come from elsewhere and which wants to learn from other people's values. In Mali the various ethnic groups have their specific identities, that are understood in our society, and not only cultural identities but professional identities as well. There are the artisans, the *griots*, the shoemakers who are called the *garangé* in Bambara, the Bozo who are generally fisherman. So all that differentiates our country from many other countries, in terms of professionalism, in terms of race, of ethnicity and things like that.

And we also transmit the message that a Malian is a courageous person, someone who wants to work, someone who wants to get ahead. And, in our songs, we also try to exhort people to work together, hand in hand. We know that we live in a country where people live very much for each other's company and society, and we try and sing about that. We try and shine some light on certain rituals and events, like wedding ceremonies, and say that in Africa, there's a solidarity between people. We have a culture, we have a civilization, and even if we haven't been to school, we still have our own values and we know how to make use of those values. We also have a past. That's very important.

You're often spoken of as the ambassadors of the handicapped and the blind. In that role, what's the message that you'd like to transmit?

AMADOU: Being handicapped is one thing, but you must realise that we all live in a world where you have to try prove your worth, and work, and make yourself useful...

MARIAM: And take courage too...

AMADOU: That's right. So we try and transmit this message about taking courage by saying that we're handicapped and we must accept it. Because the first thing you must do is accept the good and the bad of your situation. You have to accept yourself, and on that basis, try and build a future for yourself. And it is possible for us to evolve with everyone else because we're not alone, we're with everyone. So one must make connections, one must forge links. Even if people don't want to understand you have to try and make them understand. And you must say to yourself, 'I'm a member of humanity. Other people work, I have to work too.' Maybe not in the same way, but you have to find a way of adapting.

You must always have courage, you mustn't give up, we can do plenty of things. With some help, and with special services and conditions, we'll be able to integrate.

If you look at everything you've lived through, professionally, and personally, what would you have sacrificed to be given just one minute of sight?

AMADOU: Well, if I'm asked personally, I regret nothing. I would sacrifice nothing to be able to see…

MARIAM: Me neither.

AMADOU: Because I think my life was made like that. I've already seen the world, back when I was young and I still had my sight. So now, I'm used to being the way I am and I have my own world. Being able to see the world changes nothing. What changes everything is to achieve something. It's not enough to just be able to see the world, you have to have a purpose. You have to make yourself useful, and be able to work, and be able to live from your work. As soon as you can do that, I think that the rest is superfluous.

MARIAM: I agree. I've never regretted not being able to see. I still have some residual vision. As it is, I travel. I go everywhere. I meet all kinds of people, and I'm with my friends. I don't miss it.

AMADOU: Sight is a bit complicated. The fact is, you can always adapt. In our childhood, we could see a bit, but our parents were very concerned and active on our behalf. They looked after us. And we also had friends, mates, who never showed us that we couldn't see. They took us wherever they went. They described what they saw for us.

MARIAM: Even in cinemas, whilst watching films, they would tell us everything...

AMADOU: That's it. So we don't have any yearning or bitterness. There were times when people would come to us and say, 'There's this guy, a healer, who can open your eyes for you.' But we'd just say, no thanks.

MARIAM: Yes, no regrets.

Amadou Bagayoko and **Mariam Doumbia** met at an institute for young blind people in Bamako, Mali, and fell in love both musically and romantically. Following several years of performing and releasing cassettes in the their native West Africa, they went on to become stars of the international stage with a string of best selling albums including *Dimanche à Bamako* and *Welcome to Mali*. Their album *1990-1995: The Best of the African Years* is a compilation of the music they recorded in Abidjan in the early years of their career.

Idrissa Keïta was born in 1960 in Bamako, Mali. He is a writer, illustrator and musician. He has published several children's books in French and two collections of poetry in German.

Ann Wright has translated fifteen books from Spanish and French including *Motorcycle Diaries*, *The Train of Ice and Fire* and *I, Rigoberta Menchu*. She is a human rights activist and lectures on the theory and practice of civilian protection. She lives in London.

Andy Morgan recently ended a seven-year stint as manager of the Touareg rockers Tinariwen and a 29-year stretch in the music industry to concentrate on writing.

The Train of Ice and Fire
Ramón Chao
Translated by Ann Wright
ISBN: 978-1-901927-44-3
Paperback: £8.99

Colombia, November 1993: a reconstructed old passenger train is carrying 100 musicians, acrobats and artists on a daring adventure through the heart of a country soaked in violence. Leading this crusade of hope is Manu Chao with his band Mano Negra.

Manu's father Ramón Chao is on board to chronicle the journey. As the papa of the train, he endures personal discomfort, internal strife, derailments, stowaways, disease, guerrillas and paramilitaries. When the train arrives in Aracataca, the real-life Macondo of *One Hundred Years of Solitude*, Mano Negra disintegrates, leaving Manu to pick up the pieces with those determined to see this once-in-a-lifetime adventure through to the end.

'A fabulous account of a wonderfully borderline-insane trip.' – *Songlines* ★★★★★

'For Manu's growing army of admirers, the book provides a magical-realist insight into how his music has developed.' – *The Guardian*

For more information on this book
and for Route's full catalogue please visit:
www.route-online.com